When Learned Men Murder

Books by David Patterson

Exile: The Sense of Alienation in Modern Russian Letters (University Press of Kentucky, 1995)

Pilgrimage of a Proselyte: From Auschwitz to Jerusalem (Jonathan David, 1993)

The Shriek of Silence: A Phenomenology of the Holocaust Novel (University Press of Kentucky, 1992)

In Dialogue and Dilemma with Elie Wiesel (Longwood Academic, 1991)

Literature and Spirit: Essays on Bakhtin (University Press of Kentucky, 1988)

The Affirming Flame: Religion, Language, Literature (University of Oklahoma Press, 1988

Faith and Philosophy (University Press of America, 1982)

WHEN LEARNED MEN MURDER

BY DAVID PATTERSON

Essays on the Essence
of Higher Education

Published by
Phi Delta Kappa Educational Foundation

Cover design by Victoria Voelker

Library of Congress Catalog Card Number 95-71479
ISBN 0-87367-484-7
Copyright © 1996 by David Patterson
Bloomington, Indiana

For Ken

TABLE OF CONTENTS

The infamous Wannsee Conference was held on 20 January 1942 in this villa on Lake Wannsee at the southwestern edge of Berlin. This gathering of Nazi Germany's "learned men," under the leadership of Heinrich Himmler's chief deputy, Reinhard Heyrich, decided the fate of Germany's Jewish population during World War II. Inset: Reinhard Heydrich (1904-1942).

INTRODUCTION

This book is not intended to be another "scientific" study of problems in higher education. It contains no statistical analysis, no data on control groups, no information gathered from questionnaires or "objective observation" through two-way mirrors. Nor is it a specialized investigation of instructional methods, institutional organization, management skills, financial strategies, or educational psychology.

Rather, it consists of a series of reflections on various aspects of higher education that are drawn from 15 years of personal experience in the classroom, on curriculum committees, and in administrative positions. In these essays I attempt, if you will, a certain orientation in the light of grave disorientation. The reflections are an effort to retrieve a relation to a center in the aftermath of a loss of such relation, a loss that has overwhelmed education and educators.

Yet this loss is neither confined nor peculiar to education and educators; rather, it goes to the core of being human. "Man's situation, his life," José Ortega y Gasset once said, "in itself is disorientation, is being lost, and, therefore, metaphysics exists" (Ortega y Gasset 1969, p. 27). This investigation, then, has its metaphysical aspect. It is a philosophical and perhaps even a spiritual inquiry into the origins of a problem and the path toward a solution. As such, it is intended for anyone with an interest in higher education, regardless of discipline or professional training. For this reason, I have tried to use language that, while philosophical, is not overly technical or esoteric.

Following are a few of the questions I examine in these essays: What has gone wrong with higher education, and why has it gone wrong? What is highest in higher education, and how can we pursue it? What is the point of higher education? What is the role of the humanities and the liberal arts in general education? What sort of curriculum might form the basis of a good general education? And what is the nature of teaching? All of these questions are tied to larger questions of what we hold dear in life and how we go about seeking it, affirming it, and preserving it. They are questions that concern not only what we want our children to learn but what we long for them to become.

That these questions must be asked is all but self-evident. It is clear that piling up facts and figures in this "information age" has shed little light on the problems that face us. Our children continue to take the lives of one another, as well as their own lives, in record numbers. Even in the schools, where we ostensibly — but merely ostensibly — promote life, life is taken. And we have become accomplices to this murder. The question raised by Emmanuel Levinas — Do we not live by killing? (see Levinas 1985, p. 120) — haunts us, as we gaze in horror on our own hands now stained with the blood that desecrates our hallowed halls. Why have we failed so miserably, not just in raising test scores but in conveying a sense of the sanctity of human life? I believe that, in part, it is because we have not asked the right questions.

Thus in order to address these issues, I turn not to various studies and theories developed by the education professionals, as in the main these studies have added little to our understanding of higher education and the problems that concern it. Instead, I draw on the various areas of the humanities and the liberal arts in which I have worked — particularly philosophy, literature, and Jewish thought — to see what these disciplines might tell us about the relationship between the pursuit of higher education and the embrace of a higher humanity. While there may be precedent for such an approach, I think it has been tried far too little.

2

Moreover, it is time for those in the liberal arts who complain about technocrats and businessmen running the university to offer alternatives regarding how the essence of higher education might be (re)conceived. This task is formidable, and there is far more at stake than any of us can imagine. In my experience, higher education administrators are not interested in the nature of higher education or in philosophical inquiry, despite the fact that people die when such matters are ignored. Many educators, it seems, believe that a university can be improved by buying more computers, improving E-mail links, obtaining grant money, or increasing recruitment, enrollment, and retention efforts. Many believe that literary or philosophical inquiry is an incidental part of a general education requirement that you "get out of the way" so that you can go on to meet the "legitimate" requirements of your major.

Such thinking must be overcome not by adding more data to those already compiled but by changing the categories of the inquiry. One premise of this study, then, is this: *Some of the core curriculum texts of a liberal arts education can tell us something about the nature of education itself.* If these texts are selected from the humanities, then we come to another premise for this project: *Education is about what sanctifies life.* It is about the life of the soul as it unfolds in the relation to human life and to higher truth.

Having heard deans, provosts, and presidents say almost nothing about these things over the past 15 years, I fear that such ideals may have been forgotten. The difficulty, of course, does not rest solely with the administrators. Nor is it confined to the disciplines in business and technology. It pervades the liberal arts and human sciences as well, where many of us have promoted our own forms of materialistic nihilism, subjective relativism, and deadly egocentrism. If higher education, as it is pursued in the liberal arts and elsewhere, is to establish some link between knowledge and life, then the questions set forth in these essays must be addressed. And if higher education fails to establish this link, then it is neither higher, nor is it education.

The title of this book, *When Learned Men Murder,* was inspired by a historical event known as the Wannsee Conference. This conference was convened in Berlin in 1942 and conducted by Reinhard Heydrich for the purpose of working out the details in implementing the Final Solution to the Jewish problem.

Heydrich had been appointed head of the Intelligence Branch of the Nazi SS *(Schutzstaffel,* or Defense Corps) in 1934. He reported to the head of the SS, Heinrich Himmler; and Himmler reported to Hitler. However, it was Hermann Goering who signed the order sent to Heydrich on 31 July 1941, which stated:

> Complementing the task that was assigned to you on 24 January 1939, which dealt with carrying out emigration and evacuation, a solution of the Jewish problem as advantageous as possible, I hereby charge you with making all necessary preparation with regard to organizational and financial matters for bringing about a complete solution of the Jewish question in the German sphere of influence in Europe. Wherever other government agencies are involved, they are to cooperate with you. I request, furthermore, that you send me before long an overall plan concerning the organizational, factual, and material measures necessary for the accomplishment of the desired solution of the Jewish question. (Hilberg 1961, p. 262)

In keeping with the task assigned to him on 24 January 1939, Heydrich had already begun to implement this order even before he received it. When the German army invaded Russia on 22 June 1941, he had sent in their wake four killing units known as *Einsatzgruppen* to exterminate the Jews in the East. Those units were responsible for the slaughter of 1.4 million Jews.

But that was not enough. The complete implementation of the Final Solution required much more than the work of paramilitary units. In order to bring about a *final* solution, Heydrich needed the organization and cooperation of numerous government agencies. Therefore on 29 November 1941 he extended invitations to the heads of those agencies to attend a meeting so that they might consolidate their efforts to murder the Jews of Europe. The agencies represented included the civil administrations of the Occupied Territories, the Ministry of the Interior, the Ministry of Justice, the Foreign Office, the Plenipotentiary for the Four-Year Plan, the Reich Chancellery, and the Gestapo. Thus the entire German bureaucracy was brought to bear in a calculated effort to murder a people.

Now known as the Wannsee Conference, this meeting originally was scheduled for 9 December 1941, one day after the first death camp went into operation at Chelmno in Poland. However, as a result of the attack on Pearl Harbor on 7 December and America's entry into the war, the meeting was postponed until 20 January 1942. At the meeting Heydrich explained that the Jews would be isolated and used for work under conditions that would weed them out through "natural selection." The survivors, he said, would then be "treated accordingly." Those who could not work — children, the elderly, the infirm — would be killed immediately. Since the meeting was intended to address an operation that had already become an explicit part of the Nazi agenda, the meeting was concluded within a couple of hours.

What is so striking about the Wannsee Conference, as we shall see, is that it was a meeting not of depraved brutes, but of highly sophisticated, highly placed, and highly educated men. Of the fourteen men who sat down to discuss the murder of the Jews, eight held doctorates from the finest universities of Central Europe. Those universities were as interested in being technologically advanced and politically correct as are our own. Those institutions, too, were preoccupied with enrollments, funding, and successful careers. Yet the very existence of the Wannsee Conference suggests that the principles that defined the essence of higher education in those universities were not inconsistent with murder.

Were those universities in that time so very different from our own? Beyond temporal superficialities, I think not. And so we must ask a question that perhaps we are afraid to ask: Is there anything at work in our own understanding of the essence of

5

higher education today that is inconsistent with murder? In the essays that follow, I shall examine this basic question in some detail.

When Learned Men Murdered: Implications of the Wannsee Conference for Higher Education

In the summer of 1988, I attended the Remembering for the Future Conference on the Holocaust held in Oxford and London. Among the most enlightening — and most disturbing — speakers at the conference was Holocaust historian Yehuda Bauer. Enlightening because he had a keen sense of how the past implicates us in our responsibility for the future; disturbing because he made clear the failure of higher education both then and now.

Knowing that he was addressing an audience of educators, Professor Bauer pointed out that of the 14 men who gathered for the Wannsee Conference, eight held doctorates. Staggered by this fact, I looked around the auditorium at my colleagues. It occurred to me that most of us also had doctorates. I wondered: Is there anything in our system of higher education today that is essentially different from the system that educated the Nazis? If not, have we gone wrong? What have we forgotten? And why?

Near the end of the *Republic*, Plato writes:

> Each of us, neglecting all other studies, should seek after and study this thing — if in any way he may be able to learn of and discover the man who will give him the ability and the knowledge to distinguish the life that is good from that which is bad, . . . taking into account all the things of which we have spoken and estimating the effect on the goodness of his life of their conjunction or their severance. (p. 842)

In this bit of ancient wisdom we have a statement of what a student should seek from his teacher and of what a teacher should impart to his student. It suggests a form of knowledge that is intrinsically tied to a pursuit of the good, a form of knowledge that demands moral accountability of both the teacher and the student. It seems that in modern times we have forgotten this insight from Greek antiquity. And the consequences have been devastating. When the link between knowledge and the good is severed in the educational endeavor, there is nothing that, in principle, would preclude murder.

The violence that surrounds us and even invades our homes provides ample evidence for this claim. For years many of us have insisted on objective, value-free education, and then have been shocked when our children grow up to have no values. The model for the failure of modern education to maintain a link between knowledge and the good, as well as the results of that failure, can be seen in the Holocaust. This point is made starkly clear in the first novel to emerge from that event, Ka-tzetnik's *Sunrise over Hell*, first published in Tel Aviv in 1946.

In this novel, Harry Preleshnik, an inmate of Auschwitz who is modeled on his author, discovers the corpse of his friend Marcel Shafran. "Prone before his eyes," writes Ka-tzetnik, "he saw the values of all humanity's teachings, ethics and beliefs, from the dawn of mankind to this day. Marcel's carcass-face revealed to him the true face of man in the image of God. He bent, stretched out his hand and caressed the head of the Twentieth Century" (Ka-tzetnik 1977, p. 111).

The corpse that Preleshnik held in his arms was that of a *Muselmann*, a 20th-century invention that, as Emil Fackenheim (1978, p. 246) has shown, is the result of the human being's reduction to the status of an animal or a specimen devoid of every trace of anything resembling a divine image.

The values of humanity's teachings and the human image itself meet this fate not at the hands of ignorant brutes but as the result of meticulous calculations by highly educated men. For example, one survivor described in Rosenberg and Myers' *Echoes from the Holocaust* (1988) recalls seeing a Nazi who smashed the skull of a Jewish infant. A copy of Kant's *Critique of Pure Reason* protruded from the murderer's pocket. Scenes of this sort led another survivor, educator Haim Ginott, to offer a plea to educators:

> My eyes saw what no person should witness. Gas chambers built by learned engineers. Children poisoned by educated physicians. Infants killed by trained nurses. Women and babies shot and killed by high school and college graduates. So I'm suspicious of education. My request is: help your students to be human. Your efforts must never produce learned monsters, skilled psychopaths, or educated Eichmanns. Reading and writing and spelling and history and arithmetic are important only if they serve to make our students human. (Ginott 1972, p. 317)

To be made human is to be drawn into a relationship to the good; and to be drawn into such a relation is to be made responsible to and for the good of the other human being.

One can understand this survivor's suspicion of education. But do we understand why education itself is indeed suspect? Much of the current discussion of the failure of education is steeped in lamentations over how far behind we are in the areas of science, mathematics, and technology. The now famous report, *A Nation at Risk,* published by the National Commission for Excellence in Education in 1983, asserts that "our once unchallenged preeminence in commerce, industry, science, and technological innovation is being overtaken by competitors throughout the world" (p. 23). In the wake of this report, special high schools have been established for students with an aptitude for science and math, and we keep a careful eye out for any sign of improvement in test scores in these areas. But to what moral or spiritual end do we monitor these scores? Where are the special schools for students with an aptitude for ethics, philosophy, literature, or religious studies? And how many schools insist on Plato's injunction that knowledge be linked with the good?

Our generation is not the first to ignore these questions. As Max Weinreich has pointed out, very few scholars in the 1920s and 1930s raised them. Hence, says Weinreich (1946, p. 10), very few were opposed to the principles underlying the development of national socialism. Indeed, in a speech given to the students of Freiburg University on 3 November 1933, Martin Heidegger declared, "The Führer himself and he alone is German reality and German law, today and henceforth" (Fackenheim 1989, pp. 167-68). Heidegger's statement was not coerced, nor was it ever recanted. It came as part of a pattern that was already in place under the Weimar Republic that preceded the Third Reich. For example, Richard Grunberger notes that "the refusal of the universities to acknowledge Germany's military defeat and the complex of sociopolitical changes arising out of it injected unassimilable toxins into Weimar's body politic" (1971, p. 305).

The toxins injected into the body politic spread from the universities to the society and back again, so that in the institutions of higher education there soon arose the notion of *Voraussetzunglose Wissenschaft,* that is, science devoid of all presuppositions, moral and otherwise: value-free science.

Ultimately, argue George Kren and Leon Rappaport, the consequence of this innovation was that:

> the scientific mode of thought and the methodology attached to it were intrinsic to the mass killings. Quite apart from the technology, the mentality of modern science is what made the Holocaust possible. . . . The rational-abstract forms of conceptual thought required and promulgated by science provided the basis for systematic and efficient identification of people by race, transportation of large numbers to concentration points, killing, and body disposal. But the more central role of science as a mentality was in providing the inspiration and justification for these technical activities. (1980, pp. 133-34)

In addition to being a moral outrage, an attempt to murder all that is holy, and a war against the very notion of humanity, the Holocaust was a scientific wonder made possible by "higher" education. If we cling to the illusion that this "science as a mentality" has nothing to do with us, we have only to recall the radi-

10

ation testing done on thousands of unknowing victims in the United States.

However, the implications of this recent history, to which we are the heirs, go beyond a problem with science as a mentality. As Plato's insight suggests, the issue here entails a break in the connection between knowledge and morality. A consideration of the Wannsee Conference and its ramifications for our understanding of higher education will show that there is more at work here than even Plato's insight might explain.

Questions Posed by the Wannsee Conference

While the seeds for the Nazi destruction of the Jews were planted as early as 1923, with Hitler's writing of *Mein Kampf* (for example, see Hitler 1971, p. 679), the construction of the *Vernichtungsläger,* or annihilation camps, did not actually begin until the summer of 1941.

Charged with working out the details for the Final Solution to the Jewish Question, Reinhard Heydrich, Chief of the Reich Security Main Office, summoned 13 men to the Interpol offices in Berlin, at Number 56-58 Am Grossen Wannsee. The meeting had originally been planned for 9 December 1941, but it was postponed to 20 January 1942 because of the Japanese attack on Pearl Harbor. The 90-minute session was held in a large home once owned by a Jew. In attendance were Gauleiter *Doktor* Alfred Meyer of the East Ministry, Staatssekretär *Doktor* Wilhelm Stuckart of the Interior Ministry, Reichsamtsleiter *Doktor* Georg Leibbrandt of the East Ministry, Staatssekretär *Doktor* Roland Freisler of the Justice Ministry, Staatssekretär *Doktor* Josef Bühler of the Government-General, SS-Oberführer *Doktor* Karl Schöngarth of the Government-General, SS-Sturmbaumführer *Doktor* Rudolf Lange, Unterstaatssekretär *Doktor* Martin Luther of the Foreign Office, and five other less highly educated men, including the infamous murderer and expert on Jewish affairs, Adolf Eichmann.

As one can see, most of those men who gathered around a table and sipped brandy as they planned the annihilation of a people were laden with credentials. Graduates of the best universities in Central Europe, they were — by all our usual, materialistic standards — highly intelligent and quite successful pillars of their community.

What had gone wrong with the education system that conferred its highest degrees on these men? Surely something had gone wrong or these men would not have ended up at the Wannsee Conference, planning a crime that in their eyes was not a crime at all but a great service to human culture. And surely what transpired at Number 56-58 Am Grossen Wannsee on 20 January 1942 harbors a warning and a reproach for all of us who would be educators, and not only for those of us involved in Holocaust education. It is not enough to raise the issues, to pass on the information concerning what happened in the Holocaust, or even to ask how it could have happened. More than this — prior to this — we must be mindful of the principles that shape our educational endeavor. And we must ask ourselves what those principles have to do with our understanding of the essence of human beings.

Indeed, at the Wannsee Conference Heydrich "noted that this conference had been called in order to obtain clarity on questions of principle" (Arad, Gutman, and Margaloit 1981, p. 250). Among the first principles that ruled the Wannsee Conference were the ideas that there is no higher truth at work in the world but only a struggle for power; that human beings bear no spiritual or divine aspect but derive their essence from their biological and racial origins; and that one group of people may become a measure of the absolute and thus establish from within itself the justification for the extermination of another group.

One thing that all of these notions have in common is the premise that the only reality at work in the world is a material reality. In a word, then, the principle that ruled at Wannsee was a principle of idolatry. Early in the 19th century the Hasidic master Rabbi Nachman of Breslov argued that the person who is obsessed with the material domination of the world:

12

is not just enslaved to one kind of idolatry, but to every single idolatrous cult belonging to all of the seventy nations of the world. This is because all forms of idolatry are rooted in materialism. Again and again the Shekhinah [the Indwelling Presence of God] cries out in pain because of these idolatries. (Nachman 1983, p. 140)

Fackenheim (1989, p. 71) insists that "once idolatry is mentioned, there appears the specter of Auschwitz, and with it the end of the age-old Christian claim that idolatry is vanquished." Idolatry arises as soon as knowledge is divorced from the good; for when it is not tied to the good, knowledge attaches itself to various forms of the material control of the world around us, to power, wealth, and status. And, as Emmanuel Levinas (1989a, p. 78) has observed, "modern man persists in his being as a sovereign who is merely concerned to maintain the *powers of his sovereignty*. Everything that is possible is permitted."

Given the concept of *Voraussetzunglose Wissenschaft* that ruled the Weimar universities, here we can begin to see a connection between education void of moral value and the Wannsee Conference. One of the first questions that we shall address in this essay, then, is whether a principle of idolatry is at work in our own system of higher education.

If a link between knowledge and the good is to be realized in a system of higher education, then we must engage that system in a continual interrogation of its underlying principles. And we must begin by examining the nature of the link between knowledge and the good. In the *Euthyphro* Plato indicates that the good derives from the divine (1961, p. 184). Levinas (1990a) is more explicit. He writes:

The moral relation reunites both self-consciousness and consciousness of God. Ethics is not the corollary of the vision of God, it is that very vision. Ethics is an optic, such that everything I know of God and everything I can hear of His word and reasonably say to Him must find an ethical expression. (p. 17)

Like all forms of idolatry, the Nazi form led to a war against God that was waged by making war against God's Chosen. At the Wannsee Conference learned men plotted not only the murder of mothers, fathers, children, families, and communities but attacked the very concept of mother, father, child, family, and community — all of which are grounded in a notion of the good derived from the divine. While Hitler was working on *Mein Kampf*, Rabbi Abraham Isaac Kook wrote, "Betrayal of the family is a betrayal that destroys the foundations of the creation and its powers in the general world, to perfect the practical and spiritual world" (Kook 1993, p. 137). In the light of the implicit attack on this wisdom by the learned men of Wannsee, we now must ensure that the principles of higher education encompass both the practical and the spiritual. The principle of idolatry that ruled those men must not be allowed to rule us.

An older contemporary of Rav Kook, a rabbi known as the Chofetz Chaim, once said, "If a man sends his children to schools where there is no reverence for the Torah and its laws, it is as though he has sent them, God forbid, to a school for idolatry" (1992, p. 76). This does not mean that we should turn our schools into yeshivot. Nor does it mean that our teachers should become preachers. But it does mean that our teachers must convey a sense of the sanctity of human life as it is established through the linkage between knowledge and the good. It means that in our pursuit of higher education we must be wary of the principle of idolatry that ruled at the Wannsee Conference.

Education Haunted by the Ghosts of Wannsee

Why the Wannsee Conference? The answer is transparent: There the extreme consequences of idolatry among highly educated men revealed themselves. And so we arrive at the most basic issues regarding the essence of higher education to be derived from the Wannsee Conference, and we ask: What are the forms of idolatry that might underlie the principles and practices of higher education? And what is the higher essence of higher education that we should pursue?

In *I and Thou*, Martin Buber maintains that "however the history of the individual and that of the human race may diverge in other respects, they agree in this at least: both signify a progressive increase of the It-world" (1970, p. 87). In this statement Buber has in mind the increasing domination of a materialistic outlook over any sort of metaphysical conceptualization of the true and the real. Our definitions of people, for example, are increasingly determined by their ethnic origin or their economic standing; increasingly the "human" sciences reduce the human being to a creature trapped in a stimulus/response relation to his environment; and statistics are increasingly confused with truth.

The ascent of the It-world, in which both the I and the Thou are drained of life, reached its pinnacle at Wannsee. And our institutions of higher education continue to be haunted by the It. The It is steeped in numbers, and nowhere are we more enthralled by numbers than in our colleges and universities. We make our students into numbers, into test scores and credit hours. Beyond that, the knowledge we offer them is largely quantitative, materialistic, and strictly pragmatic. Conscientiously handing out questionnaires covered with numerical scales, we use numbers to measure the success of our endeavors. Very often the most meaningful measure of our success is the number of dollars our graduates are raking in, just as it has become the most meaningful measure of the success of our college presidents. Thus has the influence of the It-world progressively increased.

This aspect of higher education and its collusion with the rise of the It-world has similarities to the elements underlying the Wannsee Conference. Why did the Nazis move on the Final Solution to the Jewish Question at that particular time? According to Heinz Schirk's 1984 documentary film, *The Wannsee Conference,* one answer is that the Jews were no longer useful as hostages. They had lost their value as a currency of exchange and therefore as a means of seizing power. They were no longer a means to an end, no longer marketable.

Dr. Josef Bühler entered into the Protocol of the Conference his request that the Question be resolved first in the Government-General because there the Jews "caused constant disorder in the economic structure of the country" (Arad, Gutman, and Margaloit 1981, p. 260). The primary forces at work here — money and power — often are lures used to recruit students, as we look for increasingly clever ways to convince them that we can make them more marketable, that we can help them to sell themselves, that the knowledge we offer will give them power and prestige. At Wannsee a major step was taken toward following this logic to its terrible end, where people themselves became raw material measured according to its economic value. Mouths became mines for extracting gold, hair became a textile for the manufacture of clothing, human fat became a source of soap, and human bones were made into fertilizer. Instead of causing disorder in the economic structure, the Jews were made into a material part of that structure. And all of this was made possible by, among other things, the ways in which science and technology came together to serve business.

All too often curricular concerns are shaped solely by an interest in science, technology, and business, so that various states, as well as the nation itself, may boost their economic and political influence. According to the prevailing viewpoint today, this is how state universities should serve their states. To attain such an end, we begin by trying to convince the young that the aim of higher education is to acquire the capacity and the skills to surround themselves with things. We want them to be consumers. Whenever the rationale for a given course is called into question, the most convincing justification for it is that students can *use* the information provided in that course, where "use" means to get a job, to make money, to manipulate people, and generally to prosper in the marketplace.

But the marketplace trades not only in idols and consumer goods but in human souls. Prostitution is both the oldest profession and among the most insidious, for it means selling yourself and clambering after all that is "useful" and "realistic" at the expense of what we know to be morally good and spiritually sacred. Our institutions of higher education have themselves become high-dollar brothels, where we buy and sell ourselves and the young souls placed in our care. A good school costs $10,000 per year and requires an ACT score of 21; a better one costs $20,000 and demands a score of 23. Engaging in this numbers racket, we succumb to the illusion that only that which can be quantified can be true.

Thus we fall prey to the lie and the illusion that Holocaust author Aharon Appelfeld (1979) identifies when he says, "We had been taught to speak about the Holocaust in the language of big numbers, and no language distances you from contact [with the human being] more than such a language" (p. 21). So it was at Wannsee. The very magnitude of the operation, said Heydrich, would serve as its camouflage (Schirk film). The numbers numb us into the sleeping sickness of complacency, camouflaging and veiling the human face that cries out for our response. Those eyes that haunt us in the now familiar photos from that time — especially the eyes of the children — are precisely the thing to which the numbers blind us. Blind to those eyes, we become open to murder. "Those eyes," writes Levinas (1990a), "which are so absolutely without protection, the most naked part of the human body, nonetheless offer an absolute resistance to possession, an absolute resistance in which the temptation to murder is inscribed: the temptation of absolute negation" (p. 8).

Where power is the prime directive, the temptation is absolute negation: To have power is to have the power to destroy. If we are not to succumb to this temptation, then we must gaze into those eyes that call out to us from the human face. And we must respond to them. Wannsee teaches us that education must regain a relation to the face, which is beyond all quantification and power struggle, if it is to regain a relation to the good.

According to the *Amidah,* the daily prayer of the Jews, it is by the light of the Face of the Holy One that we receive the light and the life revealed in the Torah. And it is through the human face that we perceive that light and receive that life. "Face and discourse are tied," Levinas has pointed out. "The face speaks. It speaks, it is in this that it renders possible and begins all discourse" (1985, pp. 87-88). As the origin of discourse, the face is the origin of word and meaning, of that which sanctifies life. "The face," Levinas insists, "is what forbids us to kill" (1985, p. 86).

To reduce the human being to raw material is to render him faceless, and to render him faceless is to deprive him of his humanity. When the face is thus eclipsed by the progressive increase of the It, we grow deaf to the prohibition against murder. And when the word is thereby detached from the face, it is no longer the substance of human relation but the tool of negotiation, manipulation, and domination. The relation between one human being and another governed by a quest for the sacred — as between teacher and student, for example — is aborted for the It-orientation of public relations. In many universities the business of public relations (which translates into boosting numbers) carries a vice-presidential appointment, and the effort to present a seductive face to the public has obscured the face that Levinas invokes. In order to "sell" prospective students, we offer them what we think they want and ignore what we know they need. Or have we forgotten what is truly needful?

Have we forgotten what nourishes the life of the soul and what threatens it? Have we forgotten the dearness of those placed in our care? Have we forgotten our responsibility to and for what is sacred? If so, then this is the real ignorance, the insidious ignorance, threatening higher education. It is the ignorance of educators, of all of us who sell our souls every time we make a sale.

If we have indeed forgotten these things, then Wannsee may remind us of what we, as educators, must never forget. At the Wannsee Conference Dr. Rudolf Lange noted that the success of their operation depended on a combination of "organization, deception, and an uncompromising will to destroy" (Schirk film). When the sanctity of what is most dear in the lives of our youth is lost, this principle worms its way into the educational endeavor. It may be detected in the proclamation that the goal of education is to plunder the world of its goods and thereby "get more out of life," rather than impart more to life by developing a greater capacity for response and responsibility.

The shibboleth of "getting more out of life" is but a veil that we draw over what Levinas calls the *there is*. He describes the *there is* by saying:

> There is no longer *this* or *that*; there is not "something." But this universal absence is in its turn a presence, an absolutely unavoidable presence. It is not the dialectical counterpart of absence, and we do not grasp it through thought. It is immediately there. There is no discourse. Nothing responds to us, but this silence. (1978, p. 58)

Silence of what? The silence of meaninglessness, of a world and a humanity reduced to mere matter, where the memorandum replaces all human relation or communication. Thus "responsibility for the other," writes Levinas, "being-for-the-other, seemed to me. . . to stop the anonymous and senseless rumbling of being" (1985, p. 52). The rumbling of the mute and indifferent *there is* is the opposite of the summons that arises from the face. I am reminded of T.S. Eliot's lines in his poem, "Ash Wednesday": "No place of grace for those who avoid the face/No time to rejoice for those who walk among noise and deny the voice" (Eliot 1962, p. 64).

The rumbling noise of indifference that renders us deaf to life's outcry rolled through the conference room at Wannsee and into our halls of learning. We have little time or reason to rejoice. The voices that arise from faces turned to ash are too insistent; they demand our response and our remembrance. To be sure, both Elie Wiesel (Wiesel and de Saint-Cheron 1990, p. 155) and Primo Levi (1989, p. 31) have said that the Holocaust, to which the Wannsee Conference contributed so much, was essentially a war against memory. It was therefore a war against response and responsibility, a war against history. "Now we are writing history," said Heydrich. "And in the future the Jew will no longer appear in it" (Schirk film): no place of grace for those who avoid the face. When the face of the other human being is thus erased from our endeavor, so too is every demand for responsibility. So too is erased the face of the One who forever puts to us the first three questions put to humanity, which really amount to one question, the question of life: Where are you? Where is your brother? And what have you done? The absence of these questions from that conference room in Berlin signifies the nothingness that overshadows Wannsee. And, more than ever, this absence is felt today throughout higher education.

"For finiteness and nothingness are identical," Ludwig Feuerbach has said. "Finiteness is only a euphemism for nothingness" (1957, p. 6). What is the preoccupation with numbers, with tests and measurements, with money and power, if not a preoccupation with the finite? "Four times the Führer has announced the eradication of the Jews," boasted Heydrich. "The Führer sees himself as the Robert Koch of politics, eradicating bacteria; 537,000 have been forced out of Germany, and already 100,000 in the East have been killed" (Schirk film). Thus speaks the finite in its concern for power. But, as it is written in the Agada of the Babylonian Talmud, "blessing does not occur on those things which are weighed, measured, or counted" (*En Jacob* 1918-1922, vol. 4, p. 64).

If higher education is to be characterized by response and responsibility, then we must make a conscious effort not to allow the principles behind the Wannsee Conference to form the basis of the educational endeavor. In a word, higher education must entail those studies that amount to a blessing bestowed on life and that affirm the sanctity of all human life. "I have to answer with my life," says the Russian theorist Mikhail Bakhtin, "for what I have experienced and understood in art" (1990, p. l). And so must we, as educators, answer with our own lives for what we have encountered among the learned men of the Wannsee Conference.

Education and the Affirmation of the Sacred

In order to have a better sense of what we are answering for, let us now consider the higher essence of higher education.

Near the end of Heinz Schirk's film on the Wannsee Conference, Heydrich tells Eichmann to "be as clear as necessary and as vague as possible" in the execution of his duty. This statement is a formulation of the principle of the lie that breeds death and is directly opposed to education's quest for the truth that sanctifies life. Where the affirmation of the truth of the sacred is concerned, one must be as clear as possible and only as vague as necessary. Moreover, the clarity ruling the quest is not simply a matter of adhering to a human code.

Everything done to the Jews of Germany under the Third Reich was legal, as Heydrich himself noted at the Wannsee Conference when he announced that German living space had been "cleansed of Jews in a legal manner" (Arad, Gutman, and Margaloit 1981, p. 251). Education's affirmation of the sanctity of the human being goes beyond the subjective legalities of strictly human institutions to affirm the attachment of life to life that Henri Bergson, for one, regards as the essence of ultimate concern (1954, p. 210). Therefore, at the core of the general education curriculum must be a canon of texts that are linked, either implicitly or explicitly, to a body of *sacred* texts, to a Word from which the truth and meaning of all words are derived. If education is to affirm the sanctity of human life, then educators must be conscious of the origins of life — not just in a biological sense but in regard to the ways in which our lives are sustained by the words we invoke.

The necessity of this contact with the origins of the life of the soul is a literary motif that is both ancient and modern. One sees it, for example, in the myth of Antaeus, the son of Gaia, the Earth Mother. As long as Antaeus maintained his contact with his Mother Earth, he had the strength of all the earth. Therefore, when Hercules had to do battle with him, Antaeus could be defeated only when his contact with his origin was broken. Then,

21

of course, there is Oedipus, whose name means "lame foot," indicating a problematic contact with the earth. And in later works we encounter other lame figures, such as Shakespeare's Richard III and Melville's Captain Ahab.

In education our link with the origins of life is not only a contact with the sacred texts that lie at the origin of truth in life, but also with those human beings who have newly entered life, with children. Therefore, it is significant that the children were among the first of the designated targets in the Nazis' Final Solution to the Jewish Question. Who can forget the scene in Elie Wiesel's *Night,* where he describes his arrival at Auschwitz and a prisoner asks him how old he is? "I'm not quite fifteen yet," he replies; whereupon the prisoner informs him, "No. Eighteen" (1982*a*, p. 28). Why? Because anyone under eighteen went straight to the ovens: for the learned men of Wannsee, children were primary targets for extermination.

"It is as though the Nazi killers knew precisely what children represent to us," writes Wiesel in *A Jew Today.* "According to our tradition, the entire world subsists thanks to them" (1978, pp. 178-79). In order to grasp what Wiesel refers to here, one might recall the passage from the *Midrash Rabbah,* where we read:

> Come and see how blessed are the children by the Holy One, blessed be He. The Sanhedrin were exiled, but the *Shechinah* did not go into exile with them. When, however, the children were exiled, the *Shechinah* went into exile with them. (*Midrash Rabbah* 1961, vol. 7, p. 106)

In the *Zohar* the question is asked, "Who is it that upholds the world?" The answer: "It is the voice of tender children studying the Torah; and for their sake the world is saved" (*The Zohar* 1984, vol. 1, p. 4). And in the *Midrash on Psalms* we are told that at Sinai God asked "the sucklings and the embryos: 'Will you be sureties for your fathers, so that if I give them the Torah they will live by it, but that if they do not, you will be forfeited because of them?' They replied: 'Yes'" (*Midrash on Psalms* 1959, vol. 1, p.

125). Thus we see what, according to Jewish tradition, is at stake in our adherence to the sacred texts that underlie the highest in higher education. And we see what was lost in the miscarriage of education manifested at Wannsee. If God is the *Makom,* the Place, of the world, as we are taught in the *Midrash on Psalms* (vol. 2, p. 93), Wannsee is the place that signifies His exile from the world.

But in order to be as clear as possible and only as vague as necessary, we must press the question: What is the significance of the child in the educational enterprise? If the primary task of education is to affirm, in various ways, the sanctity of human life, then the child signifies the presence of and the accountability to the sacred. This, of course, is precisely the opposite of what the child meant to the educated murderers at the Wannsee Conference — or perhaps it is precisely what the child *did* signify for them, given their determination to annihilate not only human lives but the *sanctity* of human life. As Wiesel states it in *A Beggar in Jerusalem,* "The death of a child is the death of innocence, the death of God in the heart of man. And who does not drink deeply of this truth, who does not shout it from the rooftops, is a man devoid of heart, of God" (1970*a*, p. 99).

In addition to being the signifier of the origin of life, the child is the vessel of the future of life. But with the death of the child, the future is made dead, absent, turned back on the child himself. According to the design laid out at the Wannsee Conference, the child would no longer be the flower of youth but the broken shoot of old age, forced into a category robbed of all meaning. Simon Wiesenthal remembers, "The children of the Ghetto grew up quickly, they seemed to realize how short their existence would be. For them days were months, and months were years. When I saw them with toys in their hands, they looked unfamiliar, uncanny, like old men playing with childish things" (1976, p. 47). Through the child the promise of the past and the summons of the sacred come to meet us from the horizon of the future. But when the death of the child is plotted, as it was at Wannsee, time and eternity — every notion of a transcendent and yet immanent good — are undone. The essence of education is undermined.

For educators, this means that we must transmit the outcries of the victims of Wannsee not just because those muffled cries are themselves sacred but because, in their summons for us to bear witness to the truth, they are critical to the affirmation of the sanctity of any human life to come. Only in a response to this summons can higher education regain its essence. The pursuit of higher education derives whatever genuine significance it may have from this affirmation. The child as such is the one whom we must save, if we are to save education. For in the anti-world constructed at Wannsee the child, as such, was condemned even in the midst of rescue.

Who can forget the haunting figure of a man trying to save a child in Wiesel's *Ani Maamin:* (1973*a*, pp. 89, 91). This is an image from the anti-world that was constructed by the those who attended the Wannsee Conference. More than that, it is an image that announces to us what has been placed in our hands. We, too, have a child to carry and to preserve against a principle of death that declares that there is no higher truth, that good and evil are matters of personal inclination or cultural origin, and that there is nothing sacred in and of itself.

The notion of education as an affirmation of the sacred implies a dimension of height at work in the educational endeavor, a dimension that enters into the relation precisely through the face of the one with whom we come face to face. The face, says Levinas, "is what cannot become a content, which your thought would embrace; it is uncontainable, it leads you beyond" (1985, p. 87) — beyond and upward. The face summons us to an affirmation of the sacred and puts the *higher* into higher education. "Height," Levinas explains, "introduces a sense into being. It is already lived across the experience of the human body. It leads human societies to raise up altars. It is not because men, through their bodies, have an experience of the vertical that the human is placed under the sign of height; because human being is ordained to height the human body is placed in a space in which the high and the low are distinguished and the sky is discovered" (1987*a*, p. 100). Because the child opens up to us the sacred placed in our care, the child opens up this dimension of height in the process of teaching. This is why Wiesel declares, "The Jewish children: they haunt my writings" (1982*b*, p. 10). This is why his character Abraham in *Ani Maamin* asserts, "These children/Have taken your countenance, /O God" (1973*a*, p. 57).

The dimension of height in higher education is the dimension of truth, within which the child may take on the countenance of the Most High and through which we determine our higher accountability. In its linkage with the child, the higher truth is a *living* truth, so that our responsibility to and for that truth is what decides life and death. At Wannsee the "higher" truth was the word of the Führer, which comes not from on high but from Berlin; it was therefore neither higher nor truth.

The highest in higher education lies in the One to whom we are ultimately accountable in our concern for a living truth. Once again it may help to recall an insight from Bakhtin:

> Wherever the alibi is a prerequisite for creation and expression there can be no responsibility, no seriousness, no meaning. A special responsibility is required. . . . But this responsibility can be founded only on a profound belief in a higher truth, . . . the belief that another, higher being responds to my special responsibility, that I do not act in an utter void. Apart from this belief there can be only empty pretense. (1979, p. 179)

Where Bakhtin writes "creation and expression," we may insert "education." The essence of higher education lies in this higher responsibility. In the absence of this higher relation we are left with the glorified "technical" training, the *Voraussetzunglose Wissenschaft*, of men such as those who gathered around the table at Number 56-58 Am Grossen Wannsee. The special responsibility and the higher being that Bakhtin invokes summon education to an affirmation of the sacred, beginning with an affirmation of the sanctity of the child. And all of it is effaced, the child first of all, in Dr. Alfred Meyer's statement, for example, that "the Führer's word weighs more than any paper" and in Heydrich's assertion that the world will learn to "take the Führer at his word. Period" (Schirk film). This "Period" represents the finality of the Final Solution. It is the stone that seals the tomb from which education must finds its resurrection.

In an essay called "The Education of Character," Buber writes, "Men who have lost themselves to the collective Moloch cannot be rescued from it by any reference, however eloquent, to the absolute whose kingdom the Moloch has usurped" (1965, p. 110). Nevertheless, in the Book of Leviticus we are commanded, "You shall not give any of your children to devote them by fire to Moloch, and so profane the name of your God" (18:21). There can be no doubt that at the Wannsee Conference sophisticated, cultivated, *educated* men passed the children through fire in an offering to Moloch, the god of mammon and power. And the ritual was all the more ghastly because it was performed with all the trappings and pretense of civilization.

To the extent that we allow education to be ruled by a similar principle of idolatry, we are implicated as the unwitting acolytes of these high priests. If it should be objected that these bearers of doctorate degrees offered up not their own children but the children of people they deemed parasites and vermin, we have only to point out Dr. Wilhelm Stuckart's remark at the close of the Conference. Having failed in his argument to save the *Mischlinge* from the definition of the Jew, he asked to be relieved of his duties, saying, "Some things are better left to the younger generation" (Schirk film). What, we now ask, shall we bequeath to our own younger generation as we guide them through the halls of higher education?

In our effort to respond to this question that implicates us in our responsibility, we might recall the rest of the statement from Buber's "The Education of Character" that was cited above: "One must begin by pointing to that sphere where man himself, in the hour of utter solitude, occasionally becomes aware of the disease through sudden pain" (1965, p. 110). The sudden pain here is the pain of self-recognition that comes with self-implication. It is the pain of an aging Dorian Gray as he collides with his portrait. Of course, the path toward what is most needful must be found not in the accusation of the other but in the endeavor to become an example of what we have understood to be most needful. This means that those of us who are teachers must leave behind all "objectivity," if "objectivity" means maintaining the aloof distance of indifference rather than the genuine objectivity that comes with listening to another's viewpoint.

We may choose to flee to the fixed formulas and ready answers of the materialism and consumerism that consume the soul, or we may respond with our own lives — and at times at the risk of our own lives — in an affirmation of the sacred. There is no third alternative. Standing in the shadow of Wannsee, we have no choice in our being called to the stand: teaching is testimony.

The affirmation of the sacred that opens up the highest in higher education makes the pursuit of education a matter of the highest importance. For what we are lies very much in what education means to us, and what education means to us now lies largely in the nature of our response to all that the Wannsee Conference signified. This is where the breath of affirmation is drawn and where the touch of consecration is felt. This is where the highest in higher education may cut a breach in the veil cast over the truth at Wannsee.

The Eclipse of the Highest in Higher Education

Before leaving behind us the lessons of the Wannsee Conference, we must bear in mind the fact that the highly educated men in attendance at the conference highly valued education. To be sure, among the measures taken in the annihilation of Jewish life was the elimination of Jewish children from the schools. This decree came in the Reich on 15 November 1938, and on 5 December 1939 Chaim Kaplan noted in his Warsaw Ghetto diary, "The conqueror is condemning us to ignorance. Jewish education of all kinds has ended in Poland" (1973, p. 82).

All of the learned men at Wannsee believed education was the key to a better way of life, to greater social and cultural awareness, and to deeper political responsibility — all the things that we continue to invoke as the ultimate purpose of education. They, too, were striving to reduce the dropout rate, rid their schools of drugs and alcohol, and enhance programs in science and mathematics. They, too, wanted to raise standards, improve test scores, and begin the educational process at an earlier age. How, then, was it possible for such highly educated men — men who to some extent resemble us in their views on education — to gather around a table and outline procedures for the extermination of an entire people? It was possible because, among other reasons, there were no assumptions at work in their views of education that were inconsistent with murder. It was possible because, among other reasons, education was ruled by a desire to "get more out of life," and not by the kind of question that Emmanuel Levinas has posed

29

as a basis for philosophical inquiry in general: Do we or do we not live by killing? (see Levinas 1985, p. 120). In short, it was possible because these highly educated men were utterly blind to what is highest in higher education.

I have invoked this example of the extremity that can overtake an educated society in order to point out the possible consequences of losing sight of what we take to be the purpose and essence of higher education. What begins as a certain philosophy of education, either explicit or implied, may end at the gates embossed with the sardonic slogan, "Arbeit Macht Frei."

The stake in addressing the issue of educational assumptions, then, goes far beyond the question of what might take place in the classroom. The seeds planted in the classroom grow to fruition in the living room, the courtroom, the hospital room, and other rooms where the dearness of life is either decided or ignored. Briefly stated, when educators lose their sense of the aim and essence of their endeavor, children die. This is no exaggeration. Education has become the primary arena for the unfolding of the struggle between life and death — sometimes all too literally, as the headlines about shootings in schools remind us. According to an ABC News report issued on 20 January 1994, the third leading cause of death among children in elementary and junior high schools is murder; they are dying at the rate of 12 per day.

Therefore we must ask ourselves: Do we bear witness to anything in the classrooms that would *in principle* preclude shootings in the halls? The matter is of immense urgency because we live in an age when the clichés that are tossed around to justify the educational endeavor contain very little that might be rejected by the 14 men who sat around the table at Number 56-58 Am Grossen Wannsee or by the perpetrators of violence who are their heirs.

Contrary to the counterfeit that many counselors and advisors would pass off as axiomatic truth, the aim of higher education is not to get more out of life but to impart more to life. What is essential to understanding anything about life's sanctity is the realization that we have only as much life as we offer to the other human being, that we are educated to serve and not to be served, to esteem the other person and not to enhance self-esteem. This is precisely the realization that comes to Nekhlyudov, for instance, in Leo Tolstoy's *Resurrection*. "Everything was simple now," it occurs to him, "because he was not thinking of what would be the result for himself — but only of what he ought to do. And, strange to say, he had no idea what to do for his own needs, but he knew beyond any doubt what he had to do for others. . . . 'Yes, to feel oneself not the master but a servant,' he said to himself, and rejoiced at the thought" (1981, pp. 296-97).

Contrary to the message we convey to our children, the aim of education is not to increase earning power but to enhance the capacity for response; it is not to improve prospects for making a living but to engender the ability to make a life. Here we also may recall a lesson learned by one of Tolstoy's characters, Ivan Ilych. In his effort to somehow return to a genuine life, Ivan Ilych reflects on "that deadly official life and those preoccupations about money, a year of it, and two, and ten, and twenty, and always the same thing. And the longer it lasted the more deadly it became. 'It is as if I had been going downhill while I imagined I was going up. And that is really what it was. I was going up in public opinion, but to the same extent life was ebbing away from me'" (Tolstoy 1960, p. 148). No one would wish on his children the fate with which Ivan Ilych collided. But if this is to be avoided, then, like Ivan Ilych, we must change the categories of our thinking.

What cries out for reform in education is not just the content of the curriculum or the methods of instruction but the very manner in which we think about education. This outcry arises from the depths of the very lives we have betrayed. It is true that, unlike the men who met at the Wannsee Conference, we have built no death camps. But we certainly have created a climate that promotes every manner of homelessness, domestic violence, street violence, racism, social disease, drug traffic, and other forms of death. Another disturbing statistic comes to mind in this connection: The leading causes of death among youngsters in their late teens are alcohol, drugs, and suicide. These are the signs of the eclipse of the highest in higher education, symptoms of something gone terribly wrong — not only with *what* we think of education but with *how* we think of education.

It is not enough to cite disturbing statistics. The very premises of our thought must be transformed. Of course, the transformation of thought that might return us to the highest in higher education is at once most difficult and most needful — most difficult because it entails a transformation of our own image of ourselves, most needful because without it we shall lose every trace of ourselves.

In deciding something about our educational assumptions, we decide something about what we hold dear. Hence, in the discussion that follows, those questions raised in connection with the nature of higher education also have a bearing on what we understand to be the value of human being. Further, it should be noted that the notion of higher education adopted here pertains not only to the university but to the general human endeavor to educate human beings. What I am addressing is not simply a higher level of instruction but a higher *sense* of what education and human beings are about. Let us begin, then, by asking: What exactly is eclipsed in the eclipse of the highest in higher education?

The Tree of Life: Education's Link to the Holy

If we are to hold education sacred, then in the process of educating people we must establish a relation to the sacred. And to do this we must ask: Why is education sacred? As long as we continue to definitively link education with earning power, with high technology and big business, with the marketplace of mammon — as long as we continue to think of education strictly in terms of the profane and the mundane — we shall never be able to establish an essential link between the value of education and the sanctity of life.

Adin Steinsaltz has argued that "holiness is first and foremost the sanctity of life. Where life abounds, holiness is at hand. 'Life' is a synonym for all that is most exalted in Creation. One of the names of God is 'the God of life.' The Torah is described as 'the Torah of life.' The Torah itself speaks of 'life and goodness' as of one and the same thing" (1988*b*, pp. 192-93). If education is to establish a connection with the good, then it must engender a link with life — not just with the so-called real life of the business world, which often is unreal, but with the life of the soul, which often is ignored. In the Western tradition the holiness that attaches itself to life is manifested both in the care and in the figure of the child. This can be found in texts as ancient as Homer's *Odyssey*, where Athena, the goddess of wisdom, guides Odysseus' son Telemachus in the guise of the teacher Mentor (1937, p. 28); or it may be seen in texts as modern as Elie Wiesel's *Night,* where the hanging of a child is treated as the hanging of the Holy One Himself (1982*a*, p. 62). Whatever the radical differences between these two examples may be, they bear a common implication for how we regard the educational endeavor.

Such examples, in fact, may help us to take our reflection on the phenomenon of education to a deeper level. If we give it more than casual thought, we may find rising up within ourselves a sense of awe at the mere existence of a school. Through its very presence the school entails a fundamental affirmation of something most precious in life and about life. The existence of a school implies that the lives of our youth are worth the devotion of our own lives, that there is something very sacred and yet extremely fragile in life that must be carefully nurtured or it will die, and that in the midst of the present there abides a future in which our most sublime aspirations, our most moving inspirations, and our most urgent questions might be decided. In short, education is a profound, even a miraculous embrace of the child, an offering up of ourselves to this sacred other who returns to us the life we seek to foster in him. What is highest in education, then, is rooted in the realization that comes to Shatov, for instance, in Dostoevsky's *The Possessed.* "There were two," it strikes him on the birth of a child, "and now suddenly there's a third —

a new human being, a new spirit, complete, such as no human hands could fashion; a new thought, a new love. It's even frightening. There's nothing greater than this in the world" (1962, p. 612). And there is nothing higher in the justification of education. The highest in higher education has its origins not in the Tree of Knowledge but in the Tree of Life.

In an essay titled "Education," Martin Buber describes the child, who is the center of educational concern, as "primal potential might." He explains, "This potentiality, streaming unconquered, however much of it is squandered, is the reality *child:* this phenomenon of uniqueness, which is more than just begetting and birth, this grace of beginning again and ever again. What greater care could we cherish or discuss than that this grace may not henceforth be squandered as before?" (1965, p. 83). As an embrace of this "primal potential might" — of this "grace" — higher education is tied to the foundations and origins of meaning in life. The infant we hold in our arms comes to us from the very edge of the origin, and from the depths of those eyes that take their first look at life arises the summons to affirm the dearness of life. "Because this human being exists," says Buber, "meaninglessness, however hard pressed you are by it, cannot be the real truth. Because this human being exists, in the darkness the light lies hidden, in fear salvation, and in the callousness of one's fellow-men the Great Love" (p. 98). The Great Love of what? The Great Love of the holy, which sanctifies the life of this human being.

The purpose of education, then, is not merely to impart new knowledge for its own sake but to engender a life in the future, examined and intensified by the light of the holy that is prior to all knowledge. Indeed, the light of the holy is the light created on the first utterance of the Creation. And, as Menachem Schneerson (1986) has argued, that first utterance of "Let there be light" reveals to us the mission of all who come from the hand of the Creator: it is to turn darkness into light (pp. 4-5). This also is the meaning of education. The school in our midst and the children in the school constitute a light in the midst of a world that is otherwise dark.

As the ground of meaning, that light is directed not only toward the sediment of the past but also toward the surge of the future. Both primal *and* potential, the child who harbors the highest in education lends meaning to life through a revelation of possibility and responsibility that must be decided in the realm of the *yet to be*. Indeed, for the living individual, whose life is characterized by a process of becoming, this open-ended future is just where meaning lies; for this is where all mission is determined. "The definition given to me," Mikhail Bakhtin expresses it, "lies not in the categories of temporal being but in the categories of the *not-yet-existing*, in the categories of purpose and meaning, in the meaningful future, which is at odds with anything I have at hand in the past or present. To be myself for myself means yet becoming myself (*to cease becoming . . . means spiritual death*)" (1979, p. 109). In the *Tanya*, Rabbi Schneur Zalman points out that the Hebrew word for "wisdom," *chochmah,* contains the phrase *choach mah* or "the potentiality of what is." Wisdom, he argues, is "that which is not yet comprehended" (1981, p. 77). If wisdom and spiritual life distinguish the highest in higher education, then what is highest is that which takes us into the realm of this yet-to-be; it underlies the struggle of spiritual life against spiritual death and announces the stake in that struggle. What places education in the realm of the higher is precisely the spiritual concern that opens up the holy and sanctifies life, both primally and potentially.

Having said this much, we have taken the initial step in the shift from *what* we think about education to *how* we think about education. Because thought not only rules but is ruled by language, the word *education* itself undergoes a change in its ordinary usage, now assuming a depth through its linkage with the holy. In order to follow through with this shift, we might recall the teachings of the 13th-century Sufi Ibn El-Arabi of Spain. According to El-Arabi, there are three forms of knowledge:

1) intellectual knowledge, which is "only information and the collection of facts"; 2) the "emotionalism" that consists of getting in touch with and expressing your feelings; and 3) "real knowledge, which is called the Knowledge of Reality. In this form man can perceive what is right, what is true" (Shah 1968, p. 85). The first two forms — the false forms — of knowledge outlined by El-Arabi are the forms that dominate the current confusion surrounding issues in education. They can be seen in the talk about technological innovation and feeling good about one's self.

On the other hand, the knowledge of the good and the true is tied to a knowledge of the most dear, that is, of what makes human life holy. Deeming it "Knowledge of Reality," El-Arabi suggests that education entails a process of sanctifying life not just in a relative but in an absolute sense; he suggests a movement into the *inner* sanctum of learning, where, in the words of Ralph Waldo Emerson, "Within and Above are synonyms" (1965, p. 53). Here the consciousness of the past that is so essential to education is a consciousness of tradition, not as the accumulation of customs or habits but as the history of the holy and therefore as an avenue of revelation. Indeed, the man known as the first Jewish philosopher, Saadia Gaon, regards tradition, along with Torah and reason, as one of "the three sources of knowledge" of the holy (1976, p. 336). So regarded, tradition is tied not only to a reflection on the past but to a responsibility for the future.

Recalling in this connection the relation between meaning and the realm of the yet-to-be, we see that education is a process of transforming a dead past into a living future. We undertake the study of the great works of human consciousness not because they are themselves sacred (which would amount to yet another form of idolatry) but because, in their pursuit of a living truth, they are a critical link between the holy and the life that is yet to unfold. Thus the events of teaching and learning that comprise education take on their significance through their connection with the holy, with what stands *above* the interaction between teacher and student. Without this relation to the most high, the educational accent falls away from a capacity for response and focuses on a knack for regurgitation. Without this relation, silence is a void, and truth is a mere matter of fact.

How is this relation to the Tree of Life lost? It is lost in the rise of the strictly speculative and scientific thought that has come to dominate our enthrallment with technology. The loss can be traced back to Thales, the father of the Western speculative tradition, who was walking along one night gazing up at the heavens, when he suddenly fell into a hole. As he climbed out of the pit, he vowed never again to take a single step without first looking to be sure of the firm ground under his feet. Thus Western speculative philosophy was born. But what he gained with this opening of his eyes came at the expense of his vision of the heavens.

The line of this tradition that begins with the opening of the eyes of speculation can be traced from Philo, who set out to correct the Scriptures by changing the voice of God to a vision of God (see Sandmel 1971, p. 139); to Descartes, who operated in strict accordance with the "natural light" (1979, p. 26); to Husserl, who declared that "if phenomena have no nature, they still have an essence, which can be grasped and adequately determined in an immediate seeing" (1865, p. 110). What may strike us as the esoteric ruminations of such thinkers has become commonplace in our classrooms. Having consumed the fruits of the Tree of Knowledge, our eyes have been opened only to be blinded to the Tree of Life, just as Oedipus was blinded by the natural light of the god Apollo. When he is asked who blinded him, Oedipus replies, "Apollo. Apollo. Dear Children, the god was Apollo" (Sophocles 1939, p. 63).

The point here is not to get rid of the speculative thought of reason or to abandon technology. Rather, it is to acquire some awareness of how an obsession with such pursuits may threaten us in our relation to the Tree of Life, when they no longer lead us by the hand but hold us by the throat. If such thinking dominates education in its worship of science and technology — of a strictly material reality that meets the eye and nothing more — then the threat to education comes from within education itself. Let us consider, then, exactly what constitutes this threat.

The Tree of Knowledge: Education's Threat to Itself

A modern paradigm for the bankruptcy of knowledge and the emptiness of its promises can be found in the figure of Goethe's Faust. The character Faust, himself a professor, begins this 12,000-line drama by lamenting,

> Now I have studied philosophy,
> medicine and the law,
> and unfortunately, theology,
> wearily sweating, yet I stand now,
> poor fool, no wiser than I was before;
> I am called Master, even Doctor,
> and for the last ten years have led
> my students by the nose — up, down,
> crosswise and crooked. Now I see
> that we know nothing finally.

What is implied by these last words, "we know nothing finally," is that we know nothing about the life of the soul, nothing about what there is to live and die for. Thus Faust is tempted by death: "Hail, precious phial!" (Goethe 1949, p. 18). And yet there is a spiritual death with which he must wrestle throughout the course of the play in his effort to come to some wisdom that might make all the rest of his knowledge meaningful. For knowledge alone leaves him holding a flask of poison in his hand.

"On the day you eat of this fruit," God warned, "you will surely die" (Genesis 2:17). But the man and the woman ate, and yet they did not die — or did they? The consumption of the fruits of the Tree of Knowledge underlies an effort to become "as the gods" (Genesis 3:5), that is, to usurp the highest in a crowning of the self as the highest. When this occurs, of course, all responsibility to and for the good that is most high is lost — and with it

38

all relation between education and the good. What is left is not only empty pretense, as Bakhtin says (1979, p. 179), but pretentious emptiness; suddenly I am the good, or the *institution* is the good. Here knowledge — that is, the It-oriented knowledge of a strictly rationalistic, positivistic, pragmatic outlook — presents itself not only as the means of becoming like the gods but as a god unto itself.

Thus we have the idolatry that Adin Steinsaltz describes when he asserts, "The failure to free oneself from the model and to relate to the source is idolatry" (1989, p. 100). The model in this case is the material model of the world and the logical model of thought. Failing to relate these models to a higher source, we regard them not as a means to the truth but as truth itself. And so we adore them in a confusion of the map for the terrain. The Russian philosopher Lev Shestov once pointed out that the famous statement attributed to Seneca, "If you wish to subject everything to yourself then subject yourself to reason," amounts to the deadly temptation in the wilderness: "All these things shall I give unto you if you will but bow down and worship me" (1951, p. 196). Both of these assertions easily translate into the message generally peddled by our institutions of higher education.

Knowledge is power, so the pitch goes. Therefore, education is the key to success, the passport to the future, the door to a career. Bow down to us, and we shall give you the objective science, the value-free technology, and the business savvy to plunder the world of its goods. Enter the fold, and we shall give you the capacity and the skills to surround yourself with nice things. You will be respected, admired, and envied. Thus administrators, teachers, and above all students have been placed on a market of exchange, where the things bought and sold are not only the idols we pass off as consumer goods but also human souls. All too often the schools deemed to be the "good" ones are those that are good for the economy, attracting industry, grant money, and droves of bodies. The more numbers we have entered into our computers — indeed, the greater the number of the computers we have — the better we think we are. Hence we have fallen into a terrible confusion between quantity and quality: numbers mean everything. "Successful" programs are those that demonstrate "growth," and growth is nearly always measured quantitatively. And so the numbers numb us into the sleeping sickness of complacency, where we bask in the illusion of knowing something for having increased our stores of information. "O mysteriousness without mystery," echoes Buber's outcry, "O piling up of information! It, it, it!" (1970, p. 56). And for the human being who has succumbed to the number, the piling up of "it, it, it" is a prelude to death.

Where, then, lurks the death that issues from the Tree of Knowledge, the death that threatens the highest in higher education? It lies within the hallowed halls and the hollowed souls of those institutions and individuals who would foster the very thing that they threaten. It lies in the technical reasoning or "objective thought," as Kierkegaard refers to it, that "translates everything into results" and leads a person "to be deceived into becoming objective, inhumanly identifying himself with speculative philosophy in the abstract" (1941, pp. 67-68). Interested in material, quantifiable results, we hold this serpent to our breast so that we may hoard the treasures of the world. As we have already noted, the speculative outlook is indeed *specular,* eye-oriented, and, just as the fruits of the Tree of Knowledge are "pleasing to the eye" (Genesis 3:6), so are the assumptions that rule education dominated by what is pleasing to the eye, by everything that makes the marketplace what it is. In the "progressive increase of the It-world," we recall Buber's complaint (1970, p. 87), our education assumptions have transformed students into consumers — and thus into objects of manipulation — in a betrayal of education's essence.

If the holy is at work in education, then a certain form of sanctification or blessing comes to bear in the educational process. But we are taught in the Talmud, "blessing is only possible in things not under the direct control of the eye" (*Ta'anit* 8b). The betrayal of education's essence entails a betrayal of the human being who seeks an education. When we are preoccupied primarily with things that come under the control of the eye, we deprive our students of education's blessing. And so the schools become the institutions that Buber describes when he says, "Institutions are what is 'out there' where for all kinds of purposes one spends time, where one works, negotiates, influences, undertakes, competes, organizes, administers, officiates, preaches; the halfway orderly and on the whole coherent structure where, with the manifold participation of human heads and limbs, the round of affairs runs its course" (1970, p. 93). In the institutions of higher education the business of influence, competition, and organization manifests itself largely in public relations. Therefore, in many universities the business of public relations (which often translates into "recruiting") carries a vice-presidential appointment. But the effort to present a seductive face to the public eclipses our capacity to behold the face and thus to step before the countenance. In order to "sell" a prospective student, we offer him what we think he wants and ignore what we know he needs (or have we forgotten?). Entrenched in an ignorance that leads to this ignoring, we sell our souls in bartering for the bodies of our students.

However, the threat to the highest in education exceeds the marketing and recruiting efforts that are generally external to the mission of the institution, even when they are carried out within the confines of the campus. An equal if not greater threat belongs to what is internal to the institution, and it lies in the axioms that we have allowed to dominate the methods and subject matter of curriculum and instruction. We are enthralled by anything that can be experimentally evaluated, statistically tested, and pragmatically manipulated. We are scattered along the surface of what attracts the eye, unable to perceive any substance that may lie within or beyond the parameters of our tests and measurements. Education itself is evaluated by statistical standards and ACT scores, by credit hours and retention rates, by demographics and numerical values — the very elements that undermine its aims. A statement made by Dostoevsky's underground man comes to mind:

41

> Although these gentry may on certain occasions, let us
> say, bellow like oxen at the top of their lungs, and although
> this is perhaps greatly to their honor, yet, as I have said
> before, they instantly give up in the face of impossibility. Is
> impossibility, then, a stone wall? What kind of stone wall?
> Well, of course — the laws of nature, the conclusions of the
> natural sciences. (1974, pp. 12-13)

The stone wall that eclipses the horizon of possibility — and
with it the life of the soul — is made of the fixed formulas, ready
answers, and catchy slogans from the party line that displace the
human voice and therefore the human presence in the educational encounter.

Dostoevsky's underground man has still another prophetic
insight into this lie that passes itself off as self-evident truth:

> All that is needed to discover the laws of nature; then man
> will no longer be answerable for his actions, and life will
> become exceedingly easy. All human actions will, of course,
> be classified according to these laws — mathematically, like
> a logarithm table, up to 108,000 — and entered in a special
> almanac. (p. 27)

And so it has come to pass that if we have some difficulty concerning the soul, all we need to do is consult the *Handbook of
Clinical Psychology,* and the answer is provided for us. The problem, of course, lies not only in quantitative "intellectualism," to
use El-Arabi's term, but also in what he refers to in the passage
cited above as subjective "emotionalism" (Shah 1968, p. 85).
Sensing that education must be about more than information, we
grope at empty phrases, like "enhancing self-esteem" and "getting in touch with your feelings." Rabbi Steinsaltz has a helpful
insight in this connection: "We are living in an age of psycholog-
ical values. Everything is measured by the effect on one's subjective thoughts and feelings. Does it inspire one? Does it depress
one? And the spiritual life has also become dominated by the
same shallow measure" (1988a, p. 239). Spiritual life is at the
center of the process of education that revolves around the affir-

mation of the holy. However, when education is turned over to the formulas of the intellect or to the winds of emotion, spiritual life suffocates. When this occurs, whether by formula or by feeling, we are deprived of the capacity for thought and therefore of the capacity for response.

Here lies the heart of the threat to the highest in higher education as it issues from the Tree of Knowledge alone, the thing that has wormed its way into our education assumptions: It is the deprivation of responsibility. The sanctity of human life can be affirmed only to the extent that we establish an active human presence in relation to our fellow human being; and only a capacity for response, only responsibility, can generate that active presence. In his essay, "The Education of Character," Buber makes this point by saying:

> In spite of all similarities every living situation has, like a new-born child, a new face, that has never been before and will never come again. It demands of you a reaction which cannot be prepared beforehand. It demands nothing of what is past. It demands presence, responsibility; it demands you. (1965, p. 114)

From the Tree of Knowledge we gather what is prepared beforehand to fashion a mirage of the past that, we suppose, will instill us with the power to foresee the future. Even though it has never been before, we want to see it already; we are not interested in — we are afraid of — what has never been before. Thus we strive for the godlike predictability that ends by eliminating the *not yet* of meaning, so that we might release ourselves from the fear and the pain of decisiveness. But as this predictability waxes, responsibility wanes; struggling to become as the gods and assume a God's-eye view of the world, we become less human and more blind to the face that has never been before, more deaf to the voice that comes both from the face and from beyond it.

Thus we walk amid the noise of test and measurement deaf to the outcry that resounds all around us all the time. "Even in the most meaningless particle of earth and sky," writes Nikos

Kazantzakis in *The Saviors of God,* "I hear God crying out: 'Help me!'" (1960, p. 120). How much more so does the cry of the holy rise up from the souls of the young who are entrusted to us? If the summons of life should happen to penetrate our sound-proof fortress, we very often plug our ears. To answer is to answer with our own lives for how we live and what we stand for, and that is a terrifying prospect.

In the heart of the wood stands the Tree of Knowledge; and unless we awaken to where we are, we shall have no hope of being good. This awakening entails re-establishing a relation between education and the good that instills life with meaning. For if we have no sense of the ground of meaning in life, then we can have no sense of the point in higher education as a consecration of life. The threat to education is a threat to life itself. The problem that remains, then, is this: How are we to undo the threat to education? Or how are we to undertake the transformation of thought by which we may bring about a return of the highest in higher education?

The Polarity Between the Trees: Education and Meaning

"One is never happy," Jacques Lacan has written, "making way for a new truth, for it always means making our way into it: the truth is always disturbing" (1977, p. 169). As we make our way into the truth, the truth makes its way into us. This is what distinguishes knowledge of the truth from knowledge of information. As when two drops of water merge to form a third entity, the truth and the knower of the truth combine to form a new manifestation of life. When a person comes to know the truth, to borrow a phrase from Rabbi Steinsaltz, "he embraces it and is embraced by it" (1989, p. 84).

The truth is always disturbing; because coming to know the truth entails coming to know ourselves to be in error, we must become something other than what we are. It should not be surprising to find that one might meet with some difficulty in any effort to change the axioms that mold the minds of those who govern our education institutions. When a certain professor was directing the University Honors Program at Oklahoma State, for example, he attempted to improve the curriculum by setting up a one-credit freshman orientation class that would address issues pertaining to the meaning of education in its relation to meaning in life. The rationale was to provide students setting out on the path toward a higher education the opportunity to consider the point of learning and of why they are here. Although this proposal had some support from a few members of the administration, it was vetoed with the comment, "That sounds boring. I certainly wouldn't want to take such a class." In a presentation given at the 1990 meeting of the National Collegiate Honors Council, I also heard a representative from Oklahoma State declare, "There is nothing that will bore students and turn them off faster than talk about the philosophy of education."

Once again we see how the cancer of consumerism eats away at the fabric of reflection that would bring anything resembling spiritual depth to the education concern; once again we encounter the eclipse of the highest in higher education. If students are bored, they might run away, the thinking goes. We must find ways to entertain them, not only in our teaching methods but in our subject matter. Education and meaning are the last things they want to discuss in the classroom. When they enter the classroom, it's show time. Thus a faculty member from one of the SUNY schools once boasted to me of the overflow enrollment in his course on pornographic literature.

On the other hand, it has been my experience that many students are eager to address questions concerning the significance of their lives and what there is to hold dear. The difficulty, I fear, is that we educators are ourselves less and less equipped to address such questions. Thus we ask: What is one to do when the uneducated — that is, those who have no notion of the affirmation of the sacred in life — are in control of the education institutions? Apart from pointing fingers, which is as futile as it is wrongheaded, we can strive to become better examples of what we understand to be needful. This means that those of us who are teachers cannot stand before a class without standing for something. We must convey not only those signs that indicate the mastery of a given subject, but, beyond that, we must become a "sign of this very giving of signs," as Levinas puts it (1981, p. 147), a witness to what is highest in higher education. Situated between the Tree of Knowledge and the Tree of Life, the teacher must become the link through which each sheds light on *this* human being.

A teacher may choose to flee to the formula, or he may choose to answer with his life. But he has no choice in the matter of whether he has been summoned to this witness stand. Drawing on the sum of what he has thus far come to understand about the sanctity of life, the teacher is placed in a position of having to respond to the life and for the life staring at him from the depths of his students' faces. Of course, such responsibility can arise only where the difference between student and teacher is transformed into a non-indifference in the way that Levinas describes it: "The difference in proximity between the one and the other, between me and my neighbor, turns into non-indifference, precisely into my responsibility. Non-indifference, humanity, the one-for-the-other is the very signifyingness of signification" (1981, p. 166). What Levinas calls "the signifyingness of signification," or the meaning of meaning, is what establishes a link between education and meaning. The polarity between the trees lies in the responsibility that characterizes my non-indifference.

And as the proximity between teacher and student intensifies, so does this polarity. Called forth precisely as the non-indifferent one, the teacher is called upon to affirm what there is to hold dear in life and thus to connect life with a notion of the sacred. However, in the realm of the marketplace, where the interest lies in entertaining students in order to boost enrollments, there is no concern for students as living souls, no testimony to the dearness of life, but only an insidious indifference toward the human

46

being. Hence the fascination with numbers breeds the indifference of numbers, and the concern for self-esteem cultivates a disregard for the other human being.

How this answerability to and non-indifference toward human life might manifest itself in the classroom is perhaps more clear in humanities courses — history, philosophy, literature, religion — than in other courses. After all, it is within the masterworks from these areas that the idea of the sacred and its connection with human life is directly addressed. But it may show up in other fields of study as well, and in quite explicit ways. "Beginning with *any* text," Bakhtin argues, "we always arrive, in the final analysis, at the human voice, which is to say we come up against the human being" (1981, pp. 252-53; italics added). Thus introducing this sort of responsibility to the sciences, for instance, could entail approaching those texts with an awareness of the human presence within the subject matter and of the implications for addressing the nature of human understanding. Physicist Werner Heisenberg exemplifies this stance when he notes, "Whenever we proceed from the known into the unknown we may hope to understand, but we may have to learn at the same time a new meaning of the word 'understanding'" (1954, p. 201). In *Atomic Theory and the Description of Nature*, Niels Bohr writes, "We are both onlookers and actors in the great drama of existence" (1934, p. 119), suggesting that what we see is tied to how we see, and how we see is shaped by what we are. And when Robert Oppenheimer describes the early days of quantum physics as "a time of creation," adding, "There was terror as well as exaltation in their eyes" (1966, p. 35), he takes us beyond the technological business of gathering data and into a realm where we must consider what there is to fear and to fear for. In this way Oppenheimer comes up against the human being who comes up against science.

What about other areas of study? When teaching other languages, for example, we might bear in mind Elie Wiesel's remark that "in taking a single word by assault, it is possible to discover the secret of creation, the center where all the threads come together" (1966, p. 166). That is to say, we may be mindful of those revelations of the world and of humanity that are couched in every language, each in its own peculiar way. One might note, for example, that the Spanish word *adios* literally means "to God"; that the Russian word for "peasant," *krestyanin,* means "bearer of the cross"; or that the German word for "mind," *Geist,* also can be translated as "spirit" and is a cognate of the English word *ghost.* I have already made use of such a method in this essay with respect to the Hebrew word, *chochmah.*

These examples alone indicate that there is more to be learned in the study of a foreign language than how to do business in Paris or how to locate a restroom in Prague. And the social sciences? Interestingly, this area of "human science" is perhaps the most distant from human beings, insofar as it embraces the illusion that there is some connection between human essence and statistical analysis — an illusion entertained at the expense of any concern for the life of the soul. Here we would do well to begin with an examination of the basic assumptions that rule these "sciences."

The subject areas mentioned here do not cover the entire curriculum of higher education, but they do compose the basis of a core curriculum in general education and therefore may form the foundation of an affirmation of the highest in higher education. Even a limited exposure to this kind of testimony may turn students themselves into witnesses and messengers who may bring a renewed spirit, a sense of the sacred, to their studies in business, engineering, education, and other academic areas. Indeed, the message conveyed is such that it transforms the listener into a messenger. As for the question of how teachers themselves might be trained to be such witnesses so that their teaching may be instilled with a sense of the sacred, to that we shall have to give a response much like Dostoevsky's reply to the question of how to bring about a genuine brotherhood among human beings: "How is it to be done? There is no way it can be done, but rather *it must happen of itself; it must be present in one's nature,* unconsciously a part of the nature of the whole race, in a word: in order for there to be a principle of brotherly love there must be love" (1988, p. 49).

In order for a polarity between the Tree of Knowledge and the Tree of Life to be established, there must be some inherent sense of the relation between the meaning of education and the dearness of life. There must be some inner affirmation that the human being *matters.* And yet, as suggested previously, the mere existence of a school would seem to affirm this inner sensibility. Becoming witnesses to the highest in higher education, then, is a matter of becoming who we are. "Always promised, always future, always loved," Levinas said, "truth lies in the promise and the love of wisdom" (1981, p. 29). And the love of wisdom is definitively tied to the love of the human being who seeks wisdom. This love is what leads us to the highest in higher education. This wisdom is what situates us between the two trees, where meaning and learning meet.

From the foregoing it may be seen that our relation to education includes the sum of the relations that shape the life of the soul: the relation of the self to itself, to other human beings, and to the Most High. What we are, what we *mean,* lies to a large extent in what education means to us. If a common core of learning has nothing in common with these levels of relation that constitute human being, if the process of learning is not connected with a general process of spiritual becoming, if education falls short of the affirmation of the sacred that would graft life onto knowledge — then the eclipse of the highest in higher education will spread. We shall dwell in that darkness that parades in the guise of light, a darkness "not of woods only and the shade of trees," as Robert Frost expresses it in "Mending Wall" (1965, p. 94). The serpent of technological "intellectualism" and shallow "emotionalism" must be refused its victory, even if that victory seems inevitable. Although we may see no prospect for success, we must nonetheless continue the outcry, else we shall lose what we are, as Elie Wiesel reminds us in a passage from *One Gener-*

ation After. It concerns one of the Thirty-Six Just Men, who continued his protest despite the dimming of all hope that he would be heard.

"Poor stranger," someone says to him. "You shout. You expend yourself body and soul. Don't you see that it is hopeless?"

"Yes, I see," replies the Just Man.

"Then why do you go on?"

"I'll tell you why. In the beginning, I thought I could change man. Today I know I cannot. If I still shout today, if I still scream, it is to prevent man from ultimately changing me" (1970*b*, p. 95).

So we also must continue to shout. This is where the breath of affirmation is drawn and where the touch of consecration is felt. This is where the highest in higher education may penetrate, if only for a moment, the stone wall of pragmatism that veils it.

The Politics of Power
at the Core of the Curriculum

An insidious but no longer subtle totalitarianism has invaded the discourse and therefore the thought surrounding the academic curriculum. Terms such as *political correctness, multiculturalism,* and *social equality* are among the shibboleths of this discourse. But its ruling premise is that political power, and not anything so naive as a search for truth or the sanctification of human life, is the driving forcing behind everything that transpires in academia.

As Harvey Mansfield has noted,

> The university is politicized, the politicizers say. But they do not recoil, appalled at their conclusion that every scholar deep down is a politician. No, they embrace it. They furthermore say, "It's necessary to replace the politics we've had up to now with our politics, or, rather, my politics." This is a claim of tyranny, somewhat disguised by the demand in the speech of the politicizers to democratize everything. (Mansfield 1991, p. 1)

While this view of the human being may be traced back to Aristotle's assertion that "man is by nature a political animal" (Aristotle 1947, p. 556), it constitutes a departure from Aristotle's emphasis on humanity in community. Instead of a joining together in community, what we have in this instance is a division into camps. It is *my* politics, Mansfield rightly points out: "I have a political agenda," runs the egocentrism of politically correct thinking, "therefore you must have a political agenda. And that means that you are a threat to me in my gender, my sexuality, my ethnic peculiarity, and my cultural distinction."

Here, of course, "cultural" has more to do with the accidents of birth or circumstance than with anything like religious, philosophical, or artistic achievement. The whole notion of achievement is undermined by the premise of political power, except the view of achievement as the achievement of *power*, rather than the achievement of insight, understanding, or wisdom. Achievement becomes having seized something for myself rather than having contributed something to others. "Positing that all values are equal," Thomas Lindsay has observed, "self-creation, rather than rational discovery, has become the postmodern standard of human dignity. Having jettisoned the conviction that there are authoritative standards of virtue and vice, equality in our rights is no longer sufficient, and must be replaced by equality in our lifestyles" (Lindsay 1993, p. 2). Self-creation, in turn, leads to an apotheosis of the self, where the absolute is measured in terms of feeling. Thus in many quarters what the wayward Faust of Goethe's drama affirmed has come to pass: "Feeling is everything."

The "postmodern" implication of this development is that thought, conviction, and responsibility mean nothing. Why? Because, apart from some chemical reaction in the brain, truth means nothing. If my feeling is absolute, then I do not have to give reasons for what I think. All I have to do is assume the power to legitimize what I feel. It has been argued by colleagues of mine, in fact, that the expectation of reasoned argument to support a point of view is nothing more than a form of patriarchal oppression. What is needed, they say, is not reason or argument but more power.

Guided by power, those who embrace this viewpoint also are guided by a disregard for the truth — even within their own call for value-free tolerance — so that their insistence on "sensitivity" is yet another among the series of lies that are used to justify the obliteration of truth. There are exceptions to the lifestyles that they would have tolerated: To be white, for example, is by definition to be racist; to be male is to be sexist; and to promote any curricular tradition or canon is to be imperialist. The corollary axioms are that only whites are racists, only males are sexists, and only patriarchal power brokers are imperialists. Implicit in the premise of political power is the corollary that the "truth" of one peculiarity (unless, of course, it is white, male, or otherwise authoritative) is as valid as the "truth" of any other peculiarity: I'm okay, you're okay, everyone (except white male imperialists) is okay. There is no universal truth that belongs to a common humanity.

When the struggle for power takes over the concern for the truth and sanctity of human beings, then the interest in the curriculum is an interest in domination or indoctrination, and not in education. Battle lines get drawn in such a way that we are left with the relativistic, narcissistic solipsism of the same engaging the same to the exclusion of anyone who does not belong to one's own self-interested group.

Those who are involved with current hiring practices in the university know that it is impossible to appoint a man to teach women's studies or an Asian to teach African-American studies. In keeping with a mode of thinking that resembles Nazi ideology, we have made race and gender into credentials, all in the name of overcoming racism and gender bias. Therefore only women may teach feminist studies, only African Americans may teach African-American studies, only Native Americans, only Chicanos, and so on. But it no longer ends there; this racist notion that knowledge is intrinsically tied to race has spilled over into other areas. Look at the announcements for jobs and fellowships in any issue of the *Chronicle of Higher Education,* and you will see that racial and gender qualifications extend beyond ethnic studies into every realm of the university.

Students also are affected by this bigotry, as more and more states determine the minimum tests scores required for scholarships on the basis of race and gender. In Oklahoma, for example, white males must score two points higher than black males on the ACT in order to qualify for state scholarship funds. In a political tearing of word from meaning, what used to be known for what it is — unjust discrimination — is now called "fairness" or "social justice." In the name of what? Not in the name of truth, since there is no truth or anything else that is sacred. No, it is in the name of power and privilege.

In this essay, then, I shall discuss the devastating impact of the politics of power on the academic curriculum. This discussion will entail a consideration of the nature of multiculturalism and political correctness and the perversion of the notion of social equality. Further, I will argue that such movements have ended in a desecration of education and a betrayal not only of our students but of the very groups that are supposedly served by the multi-culturalists.

Political Correctness and Multiculturalism

One of the difficulties in understanding the nature of political correctness and multiculturalism is that the language characterizing these movements often is one in which word and meaning have nothing to do with each other. "Animated by envy and hatred," as Russell Kirk (1992, p. 6) points out, the discourse of this ideology is aimed at stirring up the most base emotions of anyone who will listen, and not at summoning anything like sublime thought. Its purpose is not to affirm a common humanity but to insist on an essential and even hostile division between male and female, white and black, ice people and sun people, homophobes and homosexuals, and so on. Attaching the significance of any human insight to skin color, rather than to spiritual or intellectual achievement, the multicultural outlook has led to such ridiculous and irrelevant claims as "Moses was black" or "Plato was black" or "Jesus was black" — as if their race were the decisive element in these men's contributions to human life. Never mind the fact that the content of their thinking is diametrically opposed to the premises of multiculturalism. From the multicultural standpoint, what is essential is not fact or content but the renown enjoyed and the emotions evoked by these figures. Why? Because power is to be had through the appropriation of such authority figures.

The lie of the power play at work here can be seen in the fact that, in its politically correct contexts, the very term *multicultural* involves neither the multiple nor the cultural. Generally excluded from its politically correct meaning are the Hebrew, Greek, and Latin cultures that have shaped Western thought; indeed, anything European or involving a history of texts is suspect, if not illegitimate. Commenting on the Bible, which is the most influential text in the Western world, Herbert Schneidau notes that for the Yahwists "literature provided the one form in which [God] could be envisioned" (1976, p. 31). Later he adds that the chief influence of the Bible has been to "force ourselves to probe the words and forms before us in a never-ending labor" (p. 255). The aim of this never-ending labor has been to seek and to affirm a moral and spiritual ground that might serve as the basis not of a particular ethnic community but of a common human community. However, this is precisely the labor in which the anticulturalism posing as multiculturalism is unwilling to engage.

Cultural history is, above all, the history of the unending labor over texts in the interest of a higher truth, and this history is nowhere to be found among the multiculturalists. To be sure, the historical element — that element which is perhaps most critical to the notion of culture — is all but absent from multicultural curricula. If it is there, it is almost never concerned with any texts or events whose origins lie more than two or three hundred years in the past. And, as already noted, the multicultural concern is much more with the race of the authors of the texts in question than with the truth that they might embrace or deny.

Therefore, professors in the liberal arts are urged to include texts by women and minorities in all of their courses, regardless of what those texts and their contents might be. If the works of old white men should be studied, then the selection of those works must be justified, as indeed the selection of any text should be justified with respect to its role in a tradition and in the education mission. But in the case of other authors, their race or gender is itself a justification for reading their work, thus undermining the very justice in whose name we are asked to include the "underrepresented groups" — as though it were a matter of proper representation and not of higher education. The political concern with proper racial and gender representation itself places multiculturalism outside any larger historical scope or spiritual truth that might include some sense of tradition, where tradition is regarded as a sacred history, as the unfolding of the holy in time. Defined by the politics of power, multiculturalism is a form of materialism that locks its adherents into a time that is anti-historical.

The interest in history is the opposite of an interest in the temporal. Inasmuch as history seeks some *significance* to the events of time, the concern for the historical is a concern for the eternal, by which one may discover the universal in the particular — by which one may seek some truth or meaning that would link one human being with another, regardless of "cultural" peculiarity. The multicultural accent is on the external, to the exclusion of the internal life of the mind or the soul and therefore to the exclusion of the eternal. "Inwardness," in the words of Kierkegaard, is "the determinant of the eternal in man" (1944*a*, p. 134).

But the multiculturalists are among those who "deny the eternal in man," as Kierkegaard says. "That very instant 'the wine of life is drawn,' and every such individuality is demoniacal. If one posits the eternal, the present becomes a different thing from what one would have it be. One fears this, and thus one is in dread of the good" (1944*a*, p. 135). Thus, we may add, one is animated by envy of the other and by hatred of the good, which leads to contempt for the other human being. Like all forms of materialism, multiculturalism thrives on the fear that breeds envy and hatred. Fear of what? Fear of responsibility, which always entails vulnerability; fear of the spiritual and the invisible made manifest in responsibility to and for the other human being.

In its confinement to the temporal and its adoration of the material, politically correct multiculturalism amounts to a worship of what meets the eye. Making the forms and fortunes of nature into the highest court of all human value, it devalues and dehumanizes the very ones whose humanity is at stake — those who have truly suffered the injustices of racism, sexism, and other forms of bigotry. Placing all "decision" in the realm of the chance occurrences of nature, multiculturalism robs the human being of all responsibility and of all capacity for decision. Thus ethnic peculiarities have been successfully used in our law courts to defend crimes of rape and wife beating, just as they have been used to excuse poor academic performance. In a manner perfectly consistent with such travesty, the multicultural curriculum in our institutions of higher education extols difference at the expense of any higher relation to law, to academic standards, or to spiritual truth. And yet it is only such a relation that can transform difference into a non-indifference that would make the suffering of another human being matter. Such a curriculum exemplifies the "aesthetic position" that Karl Jaspers describes when he says:

> An aesthetic position wills "form." It turns against the infinite relationship of things, against what is in the background, the nebulous, the fluctuating. In it there is the urge towards objectivity in form, towards Being in a substance which can be possessed, towards the changeless over against the becoming. (1959, p. 27)

Race and gender are a perfect example of what Jaspers calls "Being in a substance which can be possessed"; they can be possessed because they can be seen. Defined by my race or by my gender, I do not have to become anything more than what I am. I am in possession of myself, accountable to no one and nothing. On the other hand, I cannot become more than what I am. Therefore I am spiritually dead.

In contrast to the stasis of a racially or gender-defined state of being, the process of becoming that distinguishes spiritual life is engendered by the development of an ever deeper capacity for response. "You know the sentence in Dostoevsky," Emmanuel Levinas reminds us:

> *"We are all guilty of all and for all men before all, and I more than the others."* This is not owing to such or such a guilt which is really mine, or to offenses I would have committed; but because I am responsible for a total responsibility, which answers for all the others and for all in the others, even for their responsibility. The I always has one responsibility *more* than all the others. (1985, pp. 98-99)

This "one responsibility more" that lays claim to me is the basis of my fundamental link to a human community, a link that transcends ethnic and gender distinctions. However, confined to the surface features of form, the multicultural demand is not for a greater capacity for response, a greater responsibility *from* oneself, but for more recognition *of* oneself. It is not a matter of respecting the basic sanctity of the human being. Rather, it is a matter of paying homage to a "cultural" authority. The multicultural rallying cry, therefore, is a shout of, "Me! Me! Me!"

From the standpoint of the politics of power, the purpose of the curriculum is not to achieve some educational end but to serve as an alibi for what is otherwise an unjustifiable power struggle. The curriculum is viewed not as a means of opening up new horizons of consciousness but as a way of covering up a political agenda in the interest of one group over another. Operating in the dative case of "to me" and "for me," the politically correct, multicultural curriculum is opposed to meaning and imprisoned in pretense. Meaning can happen only in the pursuit of a human life that is expressive of a higher relation and a higher responsibility. If cultural lineage should be invoked in the interests of education, it cannot be "just a matter of empty self-congratulation," as Adin Steinsaltz notes. Beyond that, "all lineage, and not just that of nobility, carries with it a certain responsibility" (1976, p. 60).

A cultural tradition harbors what might be called the word or the teaching of the fathers and mothers. If we are to truly stand in a relation to our cultural heritage, then we must answer with our lives for all that is good that we have received from that heritage. If we are to become the heirs to our tradition, then we must pass on what is sacred in that tradition by exemplifying it. This higher responsibility removes from the individual any inherent value of his or her specificity. Or better: It is only through a relation to what invisibly transcends the individual that individuality can take on any significance.

We might recall Jacques Lacan's argument that the human being assumes some internal substance only through a relation to an external Other, as he calls it, who is in a third position between two interlocutors. It is from this third position — a position assumed by sacred tradition, for example — that truth becomes an issue. Says Lacan, "The Other with a big 'O' is the scene of the Word insofar as the scene of the Word is always in third position between two subjects. This is only in order to introduce the dimension of Truth, which is made perceptible, as it were, under the inverted sign of the lie" (1968, p. 269). Only when the truth resides in this third position can it become an issue to which and for which all parties involved are accountable. Only when all involved are gathered in the name of such truth can education as the sanctification of life happen. Unfortunately, in the case at hand, what makes the truth "perceptible" is the lie of the multicultural Me — of women for women, Chicanos for Chicanos, and so on — that excludes a relation to anyone outside the group and therefore to the Other. Here the truth is not something I serve or seek but something that serves me and my agenda. Wherever this lie is at work, teaching is displaced by political recruiting, by the dissemination of propaganda and promises of power.

On the other hand, what does a genuine teaching entail? Levinas states it nicely when he says, "Teaching is a way for truth to be produced such that it is not my work, such that I could not derive it from my own interiority" (1969, p. 295) — or from my own

59

cultural peculiarity. Because truth resides in the third position that Lacan posits, I cannot derive it from my feelings or even from my thoughts. If I am left to the isolation of myself and my group, where the same forever engages the same, then I am left to the echo and the vanity of self-imitation, which is a form of spiritual starvation. Truth is not derived from me; rather, I am derived from the truth. Hence a true multiculturalism (if that term may still be used) would embrace the other in the midst of the same, rather than oppose the self to the other, the We to the They, as the current pseudo-multiculturalism does. True subjectivity, as Levinas has said, "is the other in the same. . . . The other in the same determinative of subjectivity is the restlessness of the same disturbed by the other" (1981, p. 25). But the proponents of political correctness and multiculturalism prefer to disturb rather than be disturbed. Instead of a stance of I-for-the-other, by which I assume depth through my affirmation of the depth and the dearness of the other human being, we have here a position of I-for-myself, which languishes before the mirror and, like Narcissus, ends by starving itself to death.

The politically correct invocation of Me as a ground unto Myself, therefore, undermines any truth or authenticity that it sets out to achieve; like most revolutions, the politically correct, multicultural revolution ultimately devours its own children. Indeed, it feeds on the misery of those whom it purports to serve, because, like most revolutions, it serves only itself. When its proponents are asked about the end they are trying to achieve, of course, they will rarely answer that they are out to achieve their own ends or to amass power for themselves. To be sure, most of them probably believe that their actions are in keeping with the liberal tradition at its best. Therefore they invoke justice, freedom, and social equality. But here, too, there are difficulties.

The Politically Correct Perversion of Social Equality

"It's fashionable today," Mansfield observes:

> to doubt the value of the great books because they do not promote equal rights against discrimination by sex, lifestyle,

and race. Another objection is that they are ethnocentric, because they're Western. You can use the second objection against the first. In no Eastern classic will the principle of equal rights be found. That principle is best argued in Western classics, authored, generally, by bourgeois white males. (1991, p. 5)

An examination of the history of ideas as it unfolds in the great books will prove the accuracy of Mansfield's statement. But, as I have suggested, the politics of power at the core of the curriculum is seldom interested in the history of ideas or in the great books. The result has been a perversion of how the notion of social equality is to be understood. Like the term *multicultural,* the fashionable phrase *social equality* has come to be characterized by empty pretense. On close examination one soon discovers that, in its current multicultural contexts, the politically correct curriculum has little to do with what may be properly understood to be either social or equitable.

Let us consider first the notion of the *social.* The lie of this term, as it is used in the politics of power, comes to light as soon as we consider the affiliation between the social and the communal. In its essence the multiculturalism of the politically correct curriculum is antithetical to the social because, given its stance of I-for-myself, it is opposed to the communal. Insisting on the essential difference between one race and another or between one sex and another, multiculturalism breeds the isolation that Dostoevsky describes when he writes in *The Brothers Karamazov*:

Everyone strives to keep his individuality, every one wants to secure the greatest possible fullness of life for himself. But meantime all his efforts result not in attaining fullness of life but self-destruction, for instead of self-realization he ends by arriving at complete solitude. All mankind in our age is split up into units. (1980, p. 279)

The truth of Dostoevsky's statement can be seen in the isolation and self-destruction that continue to plague America's ghettos and reservations, which are antithetical to the concept of community.

What belongs to the communal, and therefore to the social, entails the interrelation implied by the cognates of the word: communion, communication, community. The social arises, for example, wherever it is possible to "give a reason" for an opinion, as Mansfield notes. It arises wherever there is "some common ground, offered to convince or persuade someone else. It's not me imposing on you. Therefore free speech [which is the essence of communication] implies a community, a common citizenship" (1991, p. 3). Anything truly social, then, takes on its sense within the framework of a community. And "true community," as Martin Buber argues, "does not come into being because people have feelings for each other (though that is required, too), but rather on two accounts: all of them have to stand in a living, reciprocal relation to a single living center, and they have to stand in a living, reciprocal relation to one another" (1970, p. 94). Further, the relation to one another should express the higher relation to the single living center. This higher relation makes possible the human relation not only within a community but also between communities.

Cast in the discourse of the politics of power, multiculturalism and the curriculum it would foster fail to meet either of the criteria put forth by Buber. Since a particular political interest group — because it is political — takes itself to be its own center, it stands in no relation to the living, transcendent center that Buber invokes. Insisting on a position of I-for-myself, the politics of power at the core of the curriculum falls into the hell of selfhood that Pavel Florensky describes when he says:

> Selfhood has received what it wanted and continues to want: to be its own form of the absolute, to be independent of God, affirming itself over against God. This independence, this absolute, negative freedom of egoism, is given to it. It wanted to be solitary, and it became solitary; it wanted to feed on itself, and it became self-consuming. Henceforth there is neither God nor anything else other than itself, nothing influences it. It is 'as God.' (1970, p. 242)

Taking itself to be the absolute ground of all its values, the ethnic or political interest group cannot help but regard any other group as inherently inferior to itself.

The political interest group — again, because it is political and therefore motivated by power — is a self-interest group. As such, it must regard the other, alien human being as an enemy and not as a source of reciprocal, responsive, dialogical relation. "It demands with the use of force," as Dostoevsky once observed, "demands its rights; it wants *to be separate* — and so brotherhood does not come" (1988, p. 49). Without brotherhood there is no communion, no communication, no community to which a sense of the social might be attached. And without the relation to a single sacred center, to the *Makom* or the "Place," as it is known in Hebrew, there is no brotherhood.

This is why we divide the Ten Commandments — or better, the Ten Utterances — of God into two categories: the first five, which address the relation of *adam la Makom,* or "human to the Place," and the next five, which deal with the relation of *adam l'adam,* or "human to human." The former is the foundation of the latter, and the latter is the expression of the former. Both are required for any sense of the social to flourish. As the language of this discussion of the social suggests, a social life within a community — like the life of the soul within higher education — has a religious dimension. And it derives its religious dimension precisely from a concern for *equality:* the Ten Utterances summon every human being to a human relation expressive of the relation to the divine.

As with the term *social,* however, in the use of the term *equality* we can see a perversion at work in the politics of power. Such politics often would remove everything that smacks of religious concern or divine relation from the core of the curriculum. Very often what is insisted upon here are the "inalienable rights" without the "endowed by their Creator." However, as Rabbi Steinsaltz has correctly observed, "the only way one can find any support for the idea of equality is in a very difficult religious concept: the concept that people are born in the image of the Lord and are therefore equal" (1988*b*, p. 248).

This concept goes all the way back to the Hebrew tale of the creation of humanity, as Elie Wiesel explains:

> Why did God create one man and not more? To give us a lesson in equality and teach us that no man is superior to another, we all have the same forebearer. This is also why the clay from which he was fashioned was gathered from every corner of the universe; thus no one can claim that the world or Adam belongs to him alone. Adam belongs to all men and to each in the same degree. . . . And so that one man could not taunt another, saying: My father was greater than yours. (1976, pp. 9-10)

Of course, an important point here, as essential as it is obvious, is that Adam comes from the hand and the mouth of God. That means human equality rests on a universal human sanctity derived from an essential link between the human and the sacred, between the human and the divine, regardless of any racial or cultural peculiarity.

The problem of equality lying at the core of the curriculum should not concern the institutionalization of equal representation, equal cultures, or equal power. Rather, it should concern an affirmation of the equal sanctity of all humanity in the light of a common relation to a single origin of all that is sacred. Only through the other human being — as a *human being,* and not as a member of this group or that — do we enter into a relation with the sacred, or with the Holy One, so that *doing good* becomes an issue. For the "attributes of God," as Levinas expresses it, "are given not in the indicative, but in the imperative. The knowledge of God comes to us like a commandment, like a Mitzvah. To know God is to know what must be done" (1990*a*, p. 17). Following this line of thought, Levinas elsewhere adds:

> Before culture and aesthetics, meaning is situated in the ethical, presupposed by all culture and all meaning. Moral-

ity does not belong to culture: it enables one to judge it; it discovers the dimension of height. Height ordains being. (1987a, p. 100)

Such a position is opposed to the subjective relativism that characterizes the prevailing multicultural outlook, where being ordains height, and not the other way around. Which is to say, being part of this minority or that sex sets one person above the other. In the name of what? In the name of freedom.

Although the proponents of multiculturalism invoke the word *equality* as though it were a synonym for the word *freedom*, they cling to an anything-goes relativism that undermines the higher relation which, in turn, makes all freedom possible. Once again Dostoevsky brings to light a fundamental confusion here, saying:

> The world has proclaimed the reign of freedom, especially of late, but what do we see in this freedom? Nothing but slavery and self-destruction! For the world says: "You have desires and so satisfy them, for you have the same rights as the most rich and powerful." . . . And what follows from this right of multiplication of desires? In the rich, isolation and spiritual suicide: in the poor, envy and murder. (1980, p. 289)

There is no freedom without the meaning, morality, and responsibility that engender a common humanity and that affirm a human sanctity. And so Abraham Joshua Heschel insists, "There is no freedom without sanctity" (1955, p. 170). Without this universal ground of the sacred, by which we may assess the significance of a given culture, there can be no freedom or equality within any culture. One can see, then, that just as the notion of the social is connected with community, so is the notion of equality linked to freedom.

However, as it is used in the discourse of power politics, the concept of equality is a perversion not only of brotherhood and humanity but of freedom as well. In the words of Karl Jaspers, this discourse is "concerned only with preliminary structures, with transitional forms, with phrase making" (1957, p. 181). The preliminary structures and transitional forms of multiculturalism constitute a perversion of freedom and therefore of equality because, again, they belong to what meets the eye. As we are taught in the *En Jacob,* the Agada of the Babylonian Talmud, "Blessing does not occur on things which are weighed, measured or counted, but on things which are hidden from the eye" (IV: 64). The blessing sought in the name of social equality is freedom, but the things that are here weighed, measured, and counted are sex, skin color, and surname. "Blood is inherited," in the words of Cervantes' Knight of the Rueful Figure, "but virtue is acquired, and virtue in itself is worth more than noble birth" (1979, p. 825). In modern times a similar idea is found in one of Martin Luther King's most famous remarks: "I dream of the day when my children will be judged not by the color of their skin but by the content of their character." This is, indeed, a sublime expression of the longing for freedom — not just for my freedom but for the freedom of a sacred other.

But in its perversion of freedom the politics of power at the core of the curriculum would make the very things from which liberation is sought into the highest measures of human value: "I am important, I matter, because I am black, female, Hispanic, homosexual," and not because of anything tied to integrity, honesty, responsibility, or sanctity — all the aspects of the relation to the other human being through which we realize our freedom. In its politically correct version (or perversion), social equality is a form of the spiritual slavery that Dostoevsky describes above. And to introduce the politically correct form of multiculturalism to the curriculum would be to enslave those whom one seeks to set free.

This violation of the human being is a desecration of the sacred that abides in the human being and that forms the basis of the educational endeavor. The politics of power at the core of the curriculum thus begins by promising equality and ends by undermining education. This brings us to a third point to be considered.

The Desecration of Education

The proposition that there is something to be desecrated in education implies that there is an element of the sacred at work in it. Indeed, those who are familiar with Hebrew (a tongue associated with an *unofficial* minority) will recall that in that language the word for "education," *chinuch,* also means "consecration." To the extent that education addresses the truth and meaning of life — what there is to embrace and hold dear in life — it entails a sanctification of life by engendering a truth that transcends cultural peculiarity and therefore affirms the life of humanity in all its diversity. Here the significance of cultural distinction lies not in the distinction itself but in its capacity to articulate or to open up another avenue to the holy. Only when it is approached in this manner can the difference that threatens to isolate one human being from another be transformed into the non-indifference that alone can establish a link between one human being and another. The interest in a foreign language, like the interest in an alien culture, lies not only in its distinction from other languages but also in its capacity to make heard the silence of all tongues. Out of the depth of that silence resounds "the word within a word," as T.S. Eliot calls it, "swaddled in darkness" (1962, p. 19) and yet reaching out to overcome isolation and indifference.

Expressed one way, the aim of education is to transform difference into non-indifference. In its concern for the sacred, the interests of education are the opposite of political interests, which are driven by irreconcilable differences. Without such differences there is no basis for the power struggle that defines politics. Indeed, the words *political* and *politics* have come to indicate ulterior motives, empty phrases, and gross self-interest. On the other hand, when *caring* is at the heart of the educational endeavor, we discover not the black child or the female child but the *child as such.* For the child opens up the realm of the future, of the yet to be, from which meaning is derived and by which the already given — things like race, sex, and ethnic origin — is in itself rendered inadequate for meaning. Stated differently, the equality of human beings happens when racial and generic differences become equally insignificant. And what renders them insignificant is the unfolding of the sacred. There my responsibility is not to my race, my sex, or my sexuality but to this human being who now summons me.

What distinguishes the process of the unfolding of the sacred and the announcement of such a responsibility? For one thing, it is characterized by education's pursuit of a capacity for response, as Buber might express it, of a capability on the part of the I to say Thou in the light of a relation to a Third. On this view, a student is not finished reading a literary text, for example, until he or she has responded to it in an effort to penetrate not just what is said but the implications of what is said for our approach to a higher truth. Gathered before a text, we are gathered in the presence of Another, who is the witness and the judge of our endeavor. In the *Ethics of the Fathers* this idea is conveyed in the teaching that "if two sit together and words of the Law pass between them, the Divine Presence abides between them" (1985, p. 56). Mikhail Bakhtin expresses it by invoking "the overman, the over-I — that is, the witness and judge of every man (of every I)," who stands above all dialogical encounter (1979, p. 342). Each culture, *as a culture,* has its own history of a struggle to name this Third presence. That struggle lies at the heart of education and determines what is higher in higher education.

The politics of power at the core of the curriculum is a desecration of education because it arises in an effacement of the Third and therefore in an erasure of any responsibility for another. It is a desecration of education because it refuses the truth of human encounter by reducing all encounter to a power struggle. It is a desecration of education because, in short, it threatens the life of the soul. "The soul," Bakhtin has said, "is spirit unmanifested for itself, reflected in the loving consciousness of another (person or God)" (1979, p. 98). The higher aim of *higher* education is the development of that loving consciousness, for without it — that is, without the relation to the other and to the Third expressive of a love for the sacred — we are without the truth. "'Believe in the Truth, find yourself in the Truth, love the Truth,'" cries Florensky. "That is the voice of the Truth itself, forever resounding in the soul of the philosopher" (1970, p. 72) — and in the soul of the educator, if he or she is an educator. It is a voice that comes from within and from beyond the soul, the voice that leads the soul beyond itself and into a relation to another. Education happens precisely because the human being has been summoned by this voice, because he knows that he is not the origin and the ground of the truth, that he is faced with drawing nigh unto a life that is not his own. For want of a better term, we deem this life *spirit.*

"Spirit," says Bakhtin, "is the totality of all meaningful significance and direction in life, of all the acts issuing from itself" (1979, p. 98). Buber describes spirit as word, saying, "It is not like the blood that circulates in you but like the air in which you breathe" (1970, p. 89). Like the radiation from the Big Bang, spirit arises from an ineffable origin and reverberates all around us; like the language we speak, it follows and precedes us, summoning us from beyond and above. Just as spirit remains unmanifested, so does truth. As Edmond Jabès has put it, "Truth is always on the point of coming into being" (1990, p. 76). Truth lies not in what is already said in the texts we encounter but in the response to those texts that we are about to pursue. And the thing that places truth in this realm of the yet-to-be is the quest and questioning that distinguish education. Says Jabès:

> Every question is tied to becoming. Yesterday interrogates tomorrow, just as tomorrow interrogates yesterday in the name of an always open future. The famous "Who am I?" finds its justification only in a universal questioning of which we would be but the persistent echo. (p. 74)

However, insisting on racial isolation and ethnic segregation, the politics of power is a desecration of education because it is a desecration of that universal questioning and thus of that relation through which the loving consciousness of another (person or God) may be realized. Its concern with its own agenda is the opposite of a concern for the truth. What is missing from the politically defined curriculum is precisely this loving consciousness of the other human being, which affirms a higher relation to a Third. And it is through this higher relation that the truth of a universal questioning is introduced to the educational enterprise. When this loving consciousness is absent from our lives, we are absent from ourselves and from our fellow human beings. In its declaration of I-for-myself, the politics of power at the core of the curriculum is cast in the mode of just such an absence, of just such a nothingness.

In *Why We Can't Wait* Martin Luther King points out that "centuries ago, civilization acquired the certain knowledge that man had emerged from barbarity only to the degree that he recognized his relatedness to his fellow man" (1964, p. 140). If anyone might have wondered exactly what "we shall overcome one day," we see it in this statement: It is the barbarity that isolates one human being from another. And anything that serves to isolate one person or community from another serves the ends of barbarity. The relatedness that King invokes is not the relatedness among members of a particular race or gender or lifestyle — not a relatedness grounded in the material or the natural and sustained by power. No, it is an *essential* relatedness tied to the invisible holiness of the human being, one that precedes and makes meaningful any given encounter between people. Any curriculum that is worthy of being deemed educational must foster this relatedness. In its blindness to the sanctity of the other human being, however, the politics of power signals a reversion to the barbarity that King struggled to overcome — not through an appeal to power but in an appeal to truth. As we have seen, the politics of power proceeds by dividing people into camps, and its interest in the curriculum is to sustain that division, that barbarity.

This barbarity, moreover, is more than just some historical or prehistorical condition. It is the existential condition of being turned over to the "impersonality of the 'there is'," as Levinas describes it (1985, pp. 48-49). He adds:

> To escape the "there is" one must not be posed but deposed. . . . This deposition of the sovereignty by the ego is the social relationship to the Other. . . . I distrust the compromised word "love," but the responsibility for the Other, being for-the-Other, seemed to me . . . to stop the anonymous and senseless rumbling of being. (p. 52)

The "there is" is "The horror! The horror!" that Kurtz collides with near the end of Joseph Conrad's *Heart of Darkness* (1974, p. 111). It announces itself in the horror at a life made meaningless through the eclipse of the truth and of the good by the reign of power, which is always a reign of terror, because it is always the reign of indifference. In the politics of power the impersonality of an indifferent being manifests itself in the reduction of the individual to racial and generic characteristics, thus making people into impersonal objects. By contrast, wherever education assumes a higher aspect, it has to do not with ethnic peculiarity but with human universality, not with the color of the skin but with the sanctification of the soul. It responds to the horror with the holy.

It will be asked, do not women and minorities merit the acknowledgment of their otherness on the part of educational institutions? We should reply: Certainly. But because they are human beings who harbor a trace of the holy, and not on the basis of their being women and minorities, for that would amount to the very dehumanization that education must overcome. A study of those texts authored by members of a deprived, oppressed, or "underrepresented" group must be based on the relation of those texts to a truth concerning a life that transcends the peculiarity of any particular group. The point is not that there are not enough women and minorities represented. Rather, it is that here, too, there are voices seeking the truth and sanctifying life, voices that must be heard in the interests of education. These figures must be studied, in other words, in the light of their relatedness to humanity and to a spirituality that is reflected in the loving consciousness of another, and not because of any political interest in the formation of power factions. The wisdom and therefore the educational value of King's statement cited above lie in its reflection not on the African-American condition but on the human condition as it emerges in a general human community. Similarly, the importance of addressing Nelly Sachs' poetic outcry of "all that binds us together now is leave-taking" (1967, p. 27), to take another example, lies not in its having been uttered by a woman but in its address to the depths of the soul of any human being.

No one would argue that the works of Martin Luther King or Nelly Sachs should be excluded from the curriculum. The question is: Where should they be included and why? If such figures are to make their greatest contribution to education, then they must be studied not within a curriculum defined by the politics of power — not within the politically correct, multicultural curriculum — but in the context of that larger, ever-changing canon through which education undertakes its consecration of life. Drained of its sacramental center and turned over to the political power struggle, education is left to that barbarity which is the opposite of human relatedness. And as it goes with education, so it goes with us all.

* * *

According to the 15th-century sage, Rabbi Don Isaac Abrabanel, the Tree of Life "represents the life of truth and nobility of character," while the Tree of Knowledge "represents the evening of pleasure and opportunism" (1991, pp. 388-89). This is a distinction that roughly parallels the distinctions that I have drawn between the consecration of the soul and the struggle for power. Martin Luther King's longing for his children to be judged by the content of their character is a longing for the view of education that is tied to the love of divine truth and a sanctification of human life. The politics of power, on the other hand, is by definition an opportunism that seeks only self-gratification.

In the contexts of power, knowledge is know-how. It amounts to knowing the ropes, knowing the ins and outs, knowing whose good side to get on and whose bad side to avoid. The question concerning the politics of power at the core of the curriculum, then, is a question that raises the issue of whether the curriculum is to be a branch of the Tree of Life or of the Tree of Knowledge. The former does not necessarily exclude the latter. But where there is knowledge without life — where there is opportunity without character or know-how without truth — we are left with only the political counterfeit of a life won for oneself at the expense of the life of another.

However, grown from the soil of truth and nurtured by the light of character, the Tree of Life teaches us to live our lives by imparting life to others. In that being-for-the-other lies the essence of education.

Academic Response and Responsibility: The Confusion Among the Conservatives

In May 1993 I was asked to address a gathering of generally conservative scholars and other participants at the Salvatori Conference for Academic Excellence held in Washington, D.C. The topic on which I was to speak was "A Radical Response to Educational Malfeasance." As I mulled over what I might say, the phrase "educational malfeasance" struck me as an extremely disturbing one. And the more I reflected on it, the more disturbing it became.

Malfeasance is a public official's betrayal of the public. It means that the very one entrusted with a community's well-being has been the one to violate it. The crime is most heinous when the public official involved is an educator, since an educator signifies all that is opposed to malfeasance. If any realm might be free of such betrayal, one would think that it is the realm of education, since it is in that realm that we pursue the truth and protect the precious.

The phrase "educational malfeasance" is a terribly disturbing one, because once malfeasance invades the sanctuary of education, then nothing remains of the sacred. And yet it has come to pass. The merchants of emptiness have invaded the temple, where they poison the lives of our children before those lives have had the chance to blossom. They come not to teach but to recruit, not to educate but to indoctrinate, not to praise what is sacred but to bury it. The crime is perpetrated both wittingly and unwittingly. Among the conservatives who cry out against the crime are accomplices to the crime. And so I put it to my colleagues that May: If we who regard ourselves as conservatives are to seek a radical solution to this malignant situation, then we must be radical enough to begin with a look at ourselves.

One place to start is with the inside back cover of any issue of *Academic Questions,* the journal of the National Association of Scholars. There we find a statement of the Association's mission. The NAS, the statement reads, is:

> committed to rational discourse as the foundation of acade-
> mic life in a free and democratic society. The NAS works to
> enrich the substance and strengthen the integrity of scholar-
> ship and teaching, convinced that only through an informed
> understanding of the Western intellectual heritage and the
> realities of the contemporary world, can citizen and scholar
> be equipped to sustain our civilization's achievements. In
> the light of these objectives, the NAS is deeply concerned
> about the widening currency within the academy of perspec-
> tives which reflexively denigrate the values and institutions
> of our society. Because such tendencies are often dogmatic in
> character, and indifferent to both logic and evidence, they
> also tend to undermine the basis for coherent scholarly dia-
> logue. Recognizing the significance of this problem, the
> NAS encourages a renewed assertiveness among academics
> who value reason and an open intellectual life.

This statement is a noble one. It rightly affirms certain methods and values that are indispensable to education and scholar-
ship, and it is mindful of a genuine threat to these endeavors. But it overlooks one thing, without which everything else that it says is sheer wind. Perhaps this point is overlooked because it is too obvious to mention. If experience has taught us anything, how-ever, it is that the obvious is not always obvious.

The thing overlooked can be seen in the conspicuous absence of a certain word from the association's statement — the word *truth.* Perhaps this word has been left out for political reasons, so as not to offend anyone, for fear that it might be construed as Truth with a T writ large. After all, since the time of the Enlightenment, with the shifting of the center of consciousness from the divine to the human, it has become almost axiomatic that "there are truths but no Truth." As a result, the Western intellectual heritage has in many quarters been devoted to the elimination of the Western spiritual heritage.

Do not the likes of Karl Marx and Robert Owen, in fact, belong to the Western intellectual heritage? "The passion of the Enlightenment for abstractions, generalizations, and propositions and the hostility of the 'enlightened' to the earthy, finite, and particular," notes Franklin Littell, "have produced a contempt for history and the unique event that has increasingly devitalized the language and dehumanized the word person. Thus it has come about that the worst crimes against human persons have been calculated, scientifically mounted programs, executed in the name of 'humanity,' 'the new man,' and 'social progress'"(1986, p. 67).

In keeping with certain currents in the Enlightenment, many have attacked the spiritual heritage that has shaped the notion of the sanctity of human life in the West. A growing concern over this development was what lay behind Dostoevsky's critique of the West, for example, as well as Judaism's struggle against the Haskalah movement throughout the 19th century. Nor did Marxism and socialism arise with an attack on reason; if anything, they pursued reason to a logical, materialistic conclusion concerning the nature of reality.

John Searle is quite correct in his assertion that "the postmodern conception of the university depends in various ways on a rejection of the Western Rationalistic Tradition" (1993-94, p. 81). But if all we have are logic and evidence — that is to say, the conclusions of strictly syllogistic thought and the evidence of the eyes alone — then we may be forced to the conclusion drawn by Friedrich Nietzsche, a classicist and one of the true heirs to the Western intellectual tradition drained of its spiritual tradition. He asserts:

> It is we alone who have devised cause, sequence, for-each-other, relativity, constraint, number, law, freedom, motive, and purpose; and when we project and mix this symbol

77

world into things as if it existed "in itself," we act once more as we have always acted — mythologically. The "unfree will" is *mythology*; in real life it is only a matter of *strong* and *weak* wills."(1966, p. 29)

What we find in Nietzsche may be the nightmare that Goya anticipated when he painted his canvas, *The Dream of Reason Produces Nightmare*. Left without a higher Voice from which a higher Truth summons us, we are left to such a battle between wills, so that the NAS is led to encourage a renewed *assertiveness* of the will and not a renewed testimony of the truth. If it is indeed the case that we are engaged in a power struggle with the dogmatic academic left and nothing more, then we are playing right into their hands. If it is merely a matter of who will win the day and not of who will affirm the truth, then those who "reflexively denigrate the values of our society" have won from the outset. The question we face concerns not only how we might prevail but what we hold dear.

The aim of this essay is to examine some of the prevailing views in the conservative response to the politically correct assault on the curriculum, to determine ways in which that response might be inadequate, and to raise some questions that might suggest a more responsible direction for academic conservatives. In the course of this investigation I will show that the conservatives have generally (though not entirely) failed to address the real stake in the struggle to preserve the canon of tradition. If we can not affirm a higher responsibility to a higher truth, then any truth that we might affirm is eclipsed in a pointless struggle for power. In that event education becomes just what our opponents would make of it: an arena for the vying of one political agenda over another, not for the consecration of the soul in search of the truth.

One key to understanding these issues can be found in the battle over the curriculum and the canon of texts that constitute it. The texts that we select for our students to read and the ways in which we approach them reveal much about the principles by which we live. Therefore, let us begin with a consideration of what lies behind the conservative invocation of the canon.

The Conservative Invocation of the Canon and Tradition

On 16-18 April 1993 I attended the fourth annual meeting of the National Association of Scholars in San Francisco. As I listened to the remarks from the lectern and in the halls, I began to realize why the traditionalists of the NAS and other conservative groups have been rather ineffective in their response to the "postmodernist" malfeasance that is destroying the university.

The members of the NAS and other conservative organizations certainly have some awareness of what is threatened in the deconstruction of the canon. They see that the basis of Western thought and truth is undermined by the implementation of feminist, ethnic, and other area studies that may be taught only by women, only by people of color, and so on, where accidents of nature are regarded as academic qualifications. They understand that scholarly pursuit based on subjectivism and political power struggles inevitably succumbs to intellectual mediocrity and dishonesty. And they know that if this process of deconstruction and decay continues, then the university and a society grounded in truth, meaning, and reason will die. They see, they understand, and they know that a serious struggle is taking place. But, like their opponents, they generally have little sense of why any of this matters.

Their opponents have made an idol of egocentrism molded from the stuff of subjective relativism. Yet many among the conservatives have idols of their own and liturgies to go with them. They worship the canon, they adore intellectual excellence, and they bow down to the promises of knowledge. However, like Jews who have failed to heed their rabbi's warning, they stand before the remnant of the Western Wall, where they pray *to* the Wall, not *at* the Wall.

In his article, "The Mission of the University," Searle, for example, laments the rise of subjectivism that opposes fundamental principles of Western metaphysics, such as the notion of an independent truth and reality that may be examined by anyone employing the light of reason. He notes that "there is a deliberate and explicit attempt to politicize the university towards a more left-wing point of view" and that "the left-wing ideology in question, unlike earlier left-wing movements in the United States, rests on a rejection of traditional standards of rationality, truth, and objectivity" (1993-94, p. 83). He goes on to explain:

> A rejection of the Western Rationalistic Tradition has facilitated a certain redefinition of scholarship, a redefinition of what we are trying to do as professional intellectuals in the universities. This change is often described as a move towards "relativism," but I would be more inclined to describe it as a kind of "politically committed subjectivism." I see this as a member of the board of the National Endowment for the Humanities. We get quite a number of applications from people where it is obvious that the person wants to write a book about his or her reactions to, feelings about, and general "take" on the Renaissance, on the plight of minority novelists in the Pacific Northwest, on transvestites in London in the eighteenth century, etc. In all of these cases the idea is to write a politically correct set of subjective reactions to the phenomenon in question. (pp. 84-85)

As usual, Searle's remarks are intelligent and insightful, and his complaint is certainly a legitimate one. But if the reactions he describes as subjectivism are tied to a politically correct viewpoint, then they may not be entirely subjective, since there is an external, identifiable political agenda with which they comply. The difficulty is not that they are entirely subjective and are therefore severed from any guiding principle. Rather, it is that they are guided by the principle that there is no higher truth at work in life, to which and for which we are answerable. This opposition to accountability is what lies at the root of politically correct subjectivity.

In *The Closing of the American Mind*, Allan Bloom describes the situation that Searle addresses as one in which the politically correct are "unified only in their relativism and in their allegiance to equality. And the two are related in a moral intention. The relativity of truth is not a theoretical insight but a moral postulate" (1987, p. 25). What Bloom calls "allegiance to equality" Searle associates with "politically committed subjectivism"; *equality* here is a term used to declare the legitimacy of any feeling, opinion, or understanding of texts. Anything goes. And yet, as these two thinkers indicate, the positions identified have a political and moral sense, according to which not just *anything* goes. So-called white patriarchy, for example, the Western Rationalistic Tradition, conventional canons and methods, are all under attack by people who insist that the elimination of standards is itself a standard to follow. And inasmuch as it has the status of a standard, this opposition to the tradition has a certain (albeit perverted) objective status.

Those who object or who fail to meet with the politically correct standard are to be eliminated. Power is the principle, not just an aimless subjectivity. Such a principle is not without thought but is the legacy of one of this century's most influential thinkers, Martin Heidegger. The difficulty with the Heideggerian legacy, as Emmanuel Levinas explains it, is that "Heideggerian ontology subordinates the relationship with the Other to the relation with Being in general" and that it "remains under obedience to the anonymous and leads inevitably to another power, to imperialist domination, to tyranny" (1969, pp. 46-47). It turns out, then, that the argument is not so much rationalism versus subjectivism as it is the opposition between a rational refusal of intellectual fascism and an emotional embrace of that fascism.

In an impassioned appeal for standards of academic excellence that remain true to the Western canon and tradition, Aaron Wildavsky brings out the sort of fascism I have in mind here. He writes:

> If there is no truth outside of group identification and if truth is only the servant of power, those who have power in society will feel possessed of the right to remake universities in their own image. Hence American universities will follow the process by which many Latin American universities have become so politicized that their character changes with alterations in regime. At the point where political power and the criteria for hiring university personnel coincide, Ameri-

can higher education will have irretrievably altered its character. When the egalitarian critique of our universities changes from being only partly true, as in the past, to entirely true in the present, when, in brief, power *will* determine content, all that universities should be in an open society will be lost. (1993-94, pp. 78-79)

No argument. But, we must ask, what should universities be in an open society? And what exactly is an open society? Is it a society in which one is free to say or to teach *anything* at all, a society open to everything? Is the university, in that case, a place where anything at all can be professed or practiced? If so, then why should people like Searle, Wildavsky, and the members of the NAS complain when certain things are promoted in the university?

Unless we may appeal to a higher, sacred, and living truth, we are in no position to affirm what a university must stand for and what it must not stand for. Both immanent and transcendent, only such a truth can place the interests of justice above the interests of a licentious freedom and demand a certain ethical relation to our fellow human being. Without such a concept of truth, speaking the truth becomes an empty issue and academic freedom a confused one.

In 1993 the NAS presented the Sidney Hook Memorial Award to C. Vann Woodward, the scholar who is famous as a champion of academic freedom, which, as he views it, means being free to think the unthinkable and to discuss the unspeakable. From the standpoint of the NAS, academic freedom has come to mean freedom from the fascism of political correctness, the freedom to pursue and to study the great works of the traditional canon of the Western Rationalistic Tradition. After all, it is out of the canon of that tradition that we have the notion of academic freedom, understood as the unencumbered search for an objective truth. In a similar vein Michael McDonald explains:

> We all have a rough idea of what "academic freedom" means: in the individual context, the right of professors to test the conventional wisdom through research, no matter how unpopular and no matter where the results lead; in the

institutional context, a university's right to set itself off from the rest of society, an island of retreat for scholars who wish to live "the life of the mind." But, in the end, marking the outer bounds of academic freedom requires good judgment, courage and integrity, and these qualities are in extremely short supply in academia. (1992, p. 3)

Reflecting on McDonald's last sentence, we soon realize that academic freedom does not consist of being free to say and think whatever we want, no matter how unthinkable or unspeakable it may be. Rather, it lies in speaking the truth that we *must* speak, as we best understand it, despite our fears or embarrassment. There is no freedom without this courage and integrity. It lies in taking on a responsibility to and for the sacred, which lays claim to us and imposes a mission upon us. We may choose to embrace or to betray the mission, but we have no choice in the imposition. This imposition, this summons, implies direction; and direction implies meaning. There can be no freedom, academic or otherwise, without meaning; and there can be no meaning without a relation to the absolute that imparts significance to the contingent. This means that there can be no meaning without an ethical relation to the human being that is expressive of a higher relation.

When objectivity is invoked without the invocation of this higher relation, "knowledge *of* the Disaster," to use Maurice Blanchot's words, becomes "knowledge *as* disaster" (1986, p. 3). Littell provides evidence of this when he points out that "the application of mathematical formulae and models, the very 'objectivity' and detachment which have contributed so much in the hard sciences, have led to Auschwitz, Babi Yar, the massacre in the Katyn forest, and the atrocity at Mylai" (1986, p. 67). Venerable men such as Searle, Wildavsky, and Woodward all see that the effort to preserve the traditional canon of the Western tradition involves the preservation of objective reasoning, intellectual excellence, and academic freedom. But I have heard from them little indication of why all this matters. And I do not think the answer to this "why" is self-evident. Perhaps it once was, but no more. Sometimes we must say not only what is needful but

83

why it is needful, so that we ourselves will not forget. Let us proceed with a consideration of what is needful in our institutions of higher education, and then we shall end with an argument as to why it is needful.

The Recovery of What Is Needful

John Searle has correctly pointed out that the university is a medieval institution built on a metaphysics that came out of Athens (1993-94, p. 80). This metaphysics ruled by reason led to the development of the university as an institution that, in the words of Allan Bloom:

> provided an atmosphere of free inquiry, and therefore excluded what is not conducive or is inimical to such inquiry. It made a distinction between what is important and not important. It protected the tradition, not because tradition is tradition but because tradition provides models of discussion on a uniquely high level (1987, p. 244)

The "uniquely high" distinguishes what Bloom calls "the marvelously portentous name *the sacred*" (p. 215), even though that term itself may have been devalued. Thus the invocation of a distinction between the important and the unimportant, as well as the introduction of a dimension of height to models of discussion, implies that, along with a metaphysics of reason, there is a metaphysics of religion that characterizes the university. From ancient times, whenever the life of the soul is an issue, this metaphysics and its dimension of height is at work, whether it appears in Plato's allusion to the Upper World in his famous Allegory of the Cave or in Augustine's injunction that "since the highest good is known and acquired in the truth, and that truth is wisdom, let us enjoy to the full the highest good" (1993, p. 56).

Inasmuch as education has something to do with the life of the soul, the human endeavor to seek out the truth within the university is judged in the light of a higher good and a higher truth that transcends the university. If it is a medieval institution with its origins in Athens, the university also is a religious institution with its roots in Jerusalem. Thus, along with the development of a rational methodology, there was for a time a development of the question of why it mattered. The elimination of this theological aspect of the university has contributed much to its decay. And there are those among the conservatives who have had a hand in this.

"At the beginning of the German invasion of the United States," Bloom explains, for example, "there was a kind of scientific contempt in universities for the uncleanness of religion. It might be studied in a scholarly way, as part of the past that we had succeeded in overcoming, but a believer was somehow benighted or ill. The new social science was supposed to take the place of morally and religiously polluted teachings" (p. 215). By "German invasion" we may understand the increasing influence of thinkers such as Nietzsche and Heidegger on American intellectual life. Commenting on the thesis of Heidegger's *Being and Time,* for instance, Levinas explains, "Being is inseparable from the comprehension of Being (which unfolds in time); Being is already an appeal to subjectivity." But, he adds, this amounts to subordinating:

> the relation with *someone*, who is an existent, (the ethical relation) to a relation with the *Being of the existent,* which, impersonal, permits the apprehension, the domination of the existent (a relationship of knowing), subordinates justice to freedom. . . . In subordinating every relation with the existent to the relation of Being the Heideggerian ontology affirms the primacy of freedom over ethics. (1969, p. 45)

Responsibility, on the other hand, can be derived only from the primacy of ethics over freedom, from a good that chooses me prior to any question concerning the freedom of my choosing. Resting on the abrogation of a religious outlook and its dimension of height, the elimination of "morally polluted teachings" has resulted in the elimination of morality itself. In its place we find the emergence of a freedom, which is actually mere license, to say

85

and do and intellectually justify *anything*. And there are many among the conservatives in the university who have fallen under the inimical influence of this amoral Heideggerian thinking.

Subsequently, in many instances the members of the NAS and other conservative groups want to preserve the canon that includes such medieval philosophers as Avicenna, Maimonides, and Aquinas or such literary figures as Dante, Milton, and Dostoevsky; but, like their opponents, they are often scandalized, if not utterly offended, by anyone who takes seriously the most essential aspect of these thinkers, namely, their profound religious concern. Therefore they are not quite sure of what to do with what they have preserved when, for example, they read in Maimonides' *Guide for the Perplexed*, "The belief in the existence of angels is thus inculcated in the minds of the people, and this belief is in importance next to the belief in God's Existence; it leads us to believe in Prophecy and in the Law, as opposed to idolatry" (1956, p. 356). Or when they hear Raphael declare to Adam in Milton's *Paradise Lost*:

> To ask or search I blame thee not, for Heav'n
> Is as the Book of God before thee set,
> Wherein to read his wondrous Works.

If we tell our students that such words are not to be taken seriously, then how can we expect them to take seriously the thinkers who have uttered these words? Is our interest to lie only in aesthetics, narrowly understood as a concern with form to the exclusion of substance? Are we to teach them, therefore, that the good in life is simply what feels good? If so, then what we are left with, in the words of Norman O. Brown, "is a materialization of the spirit; instead of the living spirit, the worship of a new material idol, the book" (1966, p. 195). Once this happens, the wisdom of the sages we study is lost on us. When the book becomes an idol, it no longer leads us to a higher truth that resides elsewhere, beyond the book. Rather, it leads us to the nowhere of nihilism, where we lock ourselves up in the security of our preconceptions, afraid to engage the truth to which we must answer with our very lives, and not just with our faculty of reason.

To borrow another line from Allan Bloom, those who want to retain the texts of the canon but drain them of their content "are like a man who keeps a toothless old circus lion around the house in order to experience the thrills of the jungle" (p. 216). At the 1993 meeting of the NAS, Jeffrey Hart suggested that men such as Maimonides and Milton are smarter than we are, that their genius and creativity, not their race or gender, are worthy of the serious concern of any human being. He was right, of course, and his statement drew a round of applause. But I get the feeling that many of us pride ourselves in not being so unsophisticated as to affirm anything like the holiness of the Holy One, a belief in angels, or an embrace of the Book of God set before us — that is, in not being so foolish as these men. All of us in the conservative camp insist on preserving the textual tradition of speculation; but, like our opponents, many of us are embarrassed by the text of biblical revelation to which most of that tradition responds. Some may argue that we should study great books such as *The Guide for the Perplexed* or *Paradise Lost* or *The Brothers Karamazov* so that we may better understand something about the history of ideas that has shaped our modern world. Indeed, it will be said that just as we can benefit from knowing about the political mistakes of the past, so can we benefit from knowing about the wrong-headed ideas of the past. One does not have to believe in it to study it or to learn something from it; we need not get rid of Newton just because we have Einstein.

True enough. But, unlike the eclipse of Newton by Einstein, the elimination of the truth sought by our great religious and philosophical thinkers undermines any foundation for the pursuit of the important over the unimportant. It erases the dimension of height that enables us to determine why the study of anything matters. It obliterates the center from which human life and human endeavor derive their meaning. It is not a question of whether one thinker is right and the other is wrong. What matters here is retaining the sense of the holy that impels these men in their search and that makes of education a process of consecration — that is what must be preserved in the preservation of the traditional canon.

Levinas argues that religion, rather than ontology, "is the ultimate structure" (1969, p. 80) not because of some counterfeit comfort derived from rite and ritual but because it demands that our human relation — ethical relation and responsibility — be expressive of a higher responsibility. Similarly, Henri Bergson calls religion "life's attachment to life" (1954, p. 210) not just because of its concern with the *mysterium tremendum* but because religion insists that life *matters*.

If college professors, as some of us suppose, are too highly educated to be as small-minded as Maimonides or Milton, then they have educated themselves into the undermining of anything higher in education. With this supposition, then, begins our own version of educational malfeasance. Educational malfeasance consists not only of opening the doors of the university to subjective relativism or anti-rationalism. It also lies in the degeneration of rationalism into various forms of positivism, of objectivity into gross materialism, and of academic freedom into intellectual and even moral irresponsibility.

Bloom correctly argues that "every educational system has a moral goal that it tries to attain and that informs its curriculum. It wants to produce a certain kind of human being" (p. 26). When this moral interest is coupled with our metaphysical tradition, we have the religious concern with the good and the holy that animates the thinkers who constitute most of the traditional canon. Those who would surpass those thinkers by leaving behind the religious concern also leave behind the morality and the metaphysics that they see threatened. They leave behind not only that "certain kind of human being" that education would produce but their own humanity as well. When this happens, we come to resemble many of our liberal opponents by making education into a territorial battle geared to enlisting as many students as possible into our cause. Thus the consecration of a truth that lends meaning to life is eclipsed by a struggle for power, and soon we are more concerned with political economy and political agendas *as such* than with the human sanctity that makes such things meaningful.

Again, the sanctity of the human being implies a responsibility for humanity expressive of a higher responsibility to a divinity. It summons a structure of interrelation between what is above and what is below, exemplified, for one, by the American Declaration of Independence and vilified by such movements as Objectivism. The former affirms a holiness that is central to any human community, while the latter undermines it. Bloom notes that "a powerful attachment to the letter and the spirit of the Declaration of Independence gently conveyed, appealing to each man's reason, was the goal of the education of democratic man" (p. 27). What Bloom and many other conservative intellectuals fail to point out is that the Declaration also appeals to each man's piety, invoking as it does "nature's God," the "Creator," the "Supreme Judge of the world," and "divine Providence" (see Jefferson 1977, pp. 235-41). However, the founder of Objectivism, Ayn Rand, asserts that "the source of man's rights is man's nature" (1964, p. 94), and not the Creator or society. On this admittedly self-centered view, rights are my rights, something I must ensure for myself, not for my neighbor. When education becomes contaminated with such a view, it becomes a matter of getting more from life rather than imparting more to life, a matter of being served rather than of serving.

Thus, instead of meeting a responsibility to the Good that chooses us before we make any choices, we become interested only in winning. The danger is that we come to resemble the enemy by replacing one form of egocentrism with another or one idolatry with another. For idolatry is nothing more than the transformation of the finite into the absolute, the contingent into the transcendent; and there is nothing more finite or contingent than what Rand calls "man's nature." And nothing more fickle. Looking at the events that transpired in Europe between 1933 and 1945, one might conclude that it is man's nature to murder. Yet there were a few lights in that Kingdom of Darkness who affirmed that, if the human being has a nature, he also has a higher responsibility. The example set by the Righteous Gentiles undercuts all of Rand's philosophy and implicates all of humanity in its higher responsibility, which transcends anything we might be instinctively inclined to do.

"The sense of the transcendent," argues Abraham Joshua Heschel, "is the heart of culture, the very essence of humanity" (1978, p. 55). Neither human nature nor human reason can by itself provide the ground for a human culture, because it can never transcend itself. Nor can it, by itself, be the basis for higher education. If education is to be *higher,* then we must determine exactly what is its ground and what makes it matter. In short, we must decide what is at stake in all this.

Why Malfeasance and the Conservative Confusion Matter

In a word, what is at stake in the conflict between conservatives and liberals in higher education is not this culture or that but the very *measure* of human culture. As Heschel maintains:

> We gauge culture by the extent to which a whole people, not only individuals, live in accordance with the dictates of an eternal doctrine or strive for spiritual integrity; the extent to which inwardness, compassion, justice and holiness are to be found in the daily life of the masses. (1978, p. 9)

While Heschel invokes inwardness, it is not the inwardness of mere feeling but the inwardness expressive of a relation to a truth that is beyond the individual. There can be no community for education to serve without a central truth that transcends both the individual and the community. And there can be no education without a relation to that sacred center.

Idolatry is the insidious enemy that threatens education and that underlies educational malfeasance. And idolatry is the worship of the immanent, whether it be in the form of race, gender and sexual preference or in the form of canon, acumen, and free-speech codes. Without the higher relation that sanctifies human relation, we are left, at best, with only a caprice that passes itself off as freedom, with only a cleverness that poses as intelligence. William Bennett makes this point very eloquently when he asserts:

> The enervation of strong religious beliefs — in *both our private lives as well as our public conversations* — has demoralized society. We ignore religion and its lessons at our peril. But instead of according religion its proper place, much of society ridicules and disdains it, and mocks those who are serious about their faith. In America today, the only respectable form of bigotry is bigotry directed against religious people. This antipathy toward religion cannot be explained by the well-publicized moral failures and financial excesses of a few leaders or charlatans, or by the censoriousness of some of their followers. No, the reason for hatred of religion is because it forces modern man to confront matters he would prefer to ignore. (1994, p. 24).

What Bennett says of society and modern man applies equally to higher education and its educators, both liberal and conservative. Why do we prefer to ignore the matters to which Bennett alludes? It is not merely because we are afraid of appearing to be unsophisticated, uneducated, or superstitious. More than that, it is because we fear the uncomfortable connection between what we teach and how we live, between the texts we study and the witness we bear, between our big words and our small deeds.

Again, culture alone is not the question, although some would make it so. Many in the liberal camp promote a worship of culture for culture's sake — Third World culture, ethnic culture, women's culture, and so on — regardless of the specific nature or human contributions of a given culture. Used to describe more and more, the word *culture* has come to mean less and less. The fixation on this term is part of the subjective relativism about which Searle complains, and it is invoked on both sides of the issue. It is as if the greatest threat to the educational institution were the loss of a studious lifestyle enjoyed by professors who view students as impediments to their "work," so that this work done for the sake of a "higher culture" often comes at the expense of anything higher in education. Many in the conservative camp, who respond to their opponents with an insistence on Western or American culture, do not take seriously the spiritual ramifications and the ethical implications of such a response — as though the issue were a question of choosing one culture over another and not a truth over a lie or a way of life over a path toward death.

Very often, what Bloom has said along these lines may apply to both camps:

> When one hears men and women proclaiming that they must preserve their *culture*, one cannot help wondering whether this artificial notion can really take the place of the God and country for which they once would have been willing to die. (1987, p. 192).

The adoration of culture is among the idolatries born of deconstructionism. But can anyone imagine Jacques Derrida shouting, "Give me deconstruction or give me death"? If this strikes us as ludicrous, it is because we must take very seriously the absolute demands of the truth that deconstructionism and other forms of relativism would undermine. We must take seriously Heschel's reply to Camus' assertion that the only really serious philosophical problem is suicide (Camus 1955, p. 3). "There is only one really serious problem," says Heschel, "and that is martyrdom" (1983, p. 45). Educational malfeasance and the confusion among the conservatives matter because of this essential difference between human beings and animals: While among animals death is a natural phenomenon, for the human being death is a form of testimony; and that makes it a task.

The measure of our devotion to the truth, to the holy, to the dearness of life lies in the devotion of our lives to others, even unto death. That is the *measure* of culture that Heschel invokes, and that is precisely what anyone with merely a political agenda — liberal or conservative — erases. Nicolas Berdyaev has said that "the last achievement of the rationalized herd-mind is to try to forget about death altogether, to conceal it, to bury the dead as unobtrusively as possible" (1960, pp. 252-53). In our own time we might amend Berdyaev's insight and note that postmodern intellectuals have gone a step farther. They have deconstructed death by attempting to release us from any responsibility to the dead and for how we die. This applies both to those who would dissociate the thought of Martin Heidegger and Paul de Man, for example, from their complicity with Nazi murderers and to those who would generally divorce death from life. In doing so, they have buried, concealed, and forgotten about the holy — and with it all that is higher — as unobtrusively as possible. This is why the Jewish prayer for the dead, the *Kaddish,* derives from the Hebrew word for "holy," *kadosh.*

If Heschel is right when he asserts, "The future of all men depends upon their realizing that the sense of holiness is as vital as health" (1983, p. 101), then the sense of holiness must find its way into what is higher in higher education. That can happen only if we can acquire a sense of the dearness of the ones to whom we offer up our lives. The stake in higher education is very high indeed, because what lives or dies is not just a tradition or an institution or a movement but the soul itself, the sacred itself, even the Holy One Himself. In the Talmudic text known as the *Pesikta de-Rab Kahana* it is said that God is God as long as we are His witnesses; but when we are no longer His witnesses, God, as it were, is not God (Kahana 1975, pp. 232-33). Elie Wiesel makes this point in a more modern context: "Dostoevsky once said that if God does not exist, then everything is permitted. I say, no, if everything is permitted, then God does not exist" (1985, vol. 1, p. 371). First we have to be witnesses to what there is to hold dear — first we have to determine that not everything is permitted — and only then can we begin to approach the higher truth that is threatened at every turn by postmodernism.

Inasmuch as the confusion among the conservatives is stirred by this threat, there is reason to believe that we do have some sense of what is needful in higher education, even though we may be a bit vague on the matter of why it matters. What Rabbi Adin Steinsaltz says of the separation of the light from its source applies to this situation:

Just as light takes on existence only when it is separated from its source, so is the reality of the world meaningful only as it is cut off from its source in the Divine. The world is something distinct and real because of the gap between, because it is not lodged any longer within God but has been emanated from God. (1989, p. 35)

If the confusion among the conservatives arises as the result of a gap that has opened between truth and its origin, then we have reason to hope — but only if we are able to recognize the gap. It is not enough to declare that the truth of the Western rationalist tradition is better than the truth — or the lie — of postmodern subjective relativism. More than that, we must be able to affirm why it is better. We must be able to determine a relation to the sacred that sanctifies human life and human learning. As Bennett has insisted, we must overcome our *acedia.* He explains:

Properly understood *acedia* is an aversion to and a negation of *spiritual* things. *Acedia* reveals itself as an undue concern for external affairs and worldly things. *Acedia* is spiritual torpor; an absence of zeal for divine things. And it brings with it, according to the ancients, "a sadness, a sorrow of the world." (1994, p. 22).

The confusion among the conservatives is connected to this sorrow of the world that we experience each time read about or encounter another politically correct or deconstructionist lunacy that has wormed its way into the university. But we must do more than shake our heads in dismay, more than raise the banner of tradition. We must reintroduce to the classroom, both directly and indirectly, a zeal for divine things.

Therefore I propose a radical response, if not a radical solution, to educational malfeasance. I offer it for consideration by the conservatives for themselves, as a matter not only of political economy but of spiritual necessity. It is one that might help us to see what we conserve as conservatives, as well what the liberals liberate — or unleash — as liberals. I propose that the discourse and the action that we bring to the fray be ruled by an implicit

94

religious concern linking the education of the mind to the conse-cration of the soul.

This does not mean that the lectern should be made into a pul-pit. But it does mean that central to what we teach, whatever we teach, should be a sense of responsibility to and for the sacred that transcends all self-interest. Without this ultimate concern, without this relation to what there is to love, without this affirmation of what is precious, both within life and beyond it, educational malfeasance ultimately does not matter. Yes, the Western Ration-alistic Tradition and the canon that issues from it are essential to the academic endeavor. But equally essential is the Western Spiritual Tradition, from which we derive the sanctity of the human being that instills our academic endeavor with urgency.

Unless those of us who are on the conservative side of the issue seek to conserve this, we ourselves cannot escape the charge of subjective relativism. And we shall come more and more to resemble the nihilistic liberalism that we oppose.

The Role of the Humanities
in Higher Education

In order to discuss the role of the humanities in higher education, we should begin with a few words about the terms *humanities* and *education*. Simply stated, the humanities include the disciplines of philosophy, history, religion, art, music, literature, languages, and other areas that address the life of the soul. Indeed, the Hebrew term for "humanities," *madaey haruach*, literally means "science of the spirit." These are the areas of endeavor that explore the facets of being or spirit in its human form. The most ancient and comprehensive of these is philosophy, or the love of wisdom that generally characterizes academic pursuit and that belongs to the essence of the human image. (After all, the terminal degree conferred in these fields is the *Ph.*D.).

"In every being that is conscious of itself," Maimonides argues, "life and wisdom are the same thing" (1956, p. 74). Hence, on the most fundamental level, the humanities both arise from and seek after a life understood according to what wisdom declares to be most dear. Like the discipline of first questions, each area of the humanities, in its own way, pursues the first questions of why we live and why we die, of how to go about making a life along the path toward making a living. Therefore, the humanities constitute not just one area of study among a variety of areas; rather, they are the source of those questions that justify the academic endeavor as such. Taking us to the origins of our humanity, the humanities call on us to answer with our lives for what we have understood about the nature of these disciplines and about higher education itself.

As for the notion of education, let us assume for now that, among other things, it involves a learning process intended to enlarge the scope of the human being's presence in a human community. In its simplest form the question of the role of the humanities in higher education is a question about the relation between a category of disciplines and a process of transmitting the wisdom of those disciplines from one generation to the next. Education is one realm in which world time and life time intersect. In the educational process the past takes on a meaning from which the present and future of human life derive their significance. Because the humanities deal with the timeless — with issues of good and evil, living and dying, the human and the holy — they have a role in higher education that distinguishes them from, say, natural and social sciences, which often do not have the same concern for the history of humanity but are primarily concerned with current affairs. Thus the humanities may shape higher education in ways that other disciplines cannot.

Thus the question concerning the role of the humanities in higher education is neither as simple nor as trivial as it may seem at first glance. For this question harbors other questions concerning what *is* and what *ought to be* with respect both to the humanities and to education. And the nature of our response to these questions bears profound implications for our concept of ourselves, our responsibility to others, and our affirmation of life. Unless we have some notion of the basis and the aim of education, we cannot determine in any responsible fashion what should unfold in the halls of our institutions. The matter of accountability or responsibility will be a key concept in our treatment of the role of the humanities in higher education.

In this examination of the role of the humanities in higher education, I shall discuss a few issues pertaining to what that role is and what it ought to be, in the light of a higher responsibility. Addressing what the role of the humanities is, I shall describe where we now stand, not only as students and teachers, but as human beings. The point in considering what the role of the humanities ought to be is to identify the *not yet* that shapes the path we follow and the meaning we foster. The *ought to be* not only opens up a future, but it posits a direction that shapes the future and imparts significance to the present.

As the Russian thinker Mikhail Bakhtin has pointed out, "the definition given to me lies not in the categories of temporal being but in the categories of the *not-yet-existing,* in the meaningful future, which is at odds with anything I have at hand in the past or present" (1979, p. 109). The movement toward the not-yet-existing, Bakhtin goes on to explain, is what characterizes the process of spiritual becoming that is indispensable to human life (p. 109); and that process of becoming is perhaps most manifest in the process of learning. The very existence of higher education implies that there is something meaningful in life, that something *matters,* and the humanities constitute the most fundamental realm where that something is pursued. As Bakhtin suggests, meaning in life arises at the juncture — or at the disjuncture — between the *is* and the *ought to be.* It is in this gap, out of this lack, that the question of who we are arises and that learning therefore transpires.

Thus the interest in the role of the humanities in higher education is an interest in humanity as the bearer of meaning. In a world where the condition of humanity appears to be increasingly precarious and the presence of meaning increasingly tenuous, the stake we have in responding to this question is very high indeed. As we shall see, it is not an exaggeration to assert that lives are in the balance. Let us consider, then, what the role of the humanities is in higher education, what it ought to be, and what is at stake in all this.

The Role of the Humanities in Higher Education

In its current state, the role of the humanities in higher education is largely shaped by what higher education itself has become. Most of us have experienced a moment or two of despair over the standards, the practices, and the conditions of modern academia. Organizations have been formed, technology has been developed, and legislation has been enacted to improve the quality of education. But in many instances an interest in the humanities is conspicuously absent from the measures taken. We want to be sure that our children come to school "ready to learn," that they stay in school and off of drugs, that they become leaders in science and mathematics, and that they can "compete in a global economy." But as we examine our institutions of higher learning, we wonder whether these measures have made our learning any higher. In fact, just a brief reflection on what currently passes for a place of learning may lead some of us to echo the opening lines from Dante's *Inferno,* where he writes of going astray in life's journey and awakening in a fearful wilderness.

Indeed, the leopard, the lion, and the she-wolf that lurk in Dante's wilderness have their counterparts in contemporary higher education, where the material, the marketable, and the political feed on the souls of students and teachers alike.

This situation is what lies behind Allan Bloom's lament:

> The professors of humanities are in an impossible situation and do not believe in themselves or what they do. Like it or not, they are essentially involved with interpreting and transmitting old books, preserving what we call tradition, in a democratic order where tradition is not privileged. They are partisans of the leisured and beautiful in a place where evident utility is the only passport. Their realm is the always and the contemplative, in a setting that demands only the here and now and the active. (1987, p. 353)

If what Bloom says is even half true, then we who are in the humanities are locked into a non-utilitarian role in a place that has no place for such "frivolity." The "world of *techne*," to paraphrase Franklin Littell, "in its aversion to the mysterious and open, has sealed off the dimension of human experience" (1986, p. 13), that is, the dimension of humanity and meaning. And so we must ask: Can we remain human if the role of the humanities in higher education is regarded as frivolous because it is not utilitarian?

This is not to say that the utilitarian is itself insidious or that technology is a threat to human life. Indeed, technological inno-

vations can be very useful to students and teachers in the humanities, and putting bread on the table is as essential to the life of the
body as the pursuit of truth is to the nourishment of the soul. But
as Abraham Joshua Heschel has warned us, "a civilization that is
devoted exclusively to the utilitarian is at bottom not different
from barbarism" (1978, p. 55). One recalls the ghetto scene from
Steven Spielberg's film, *Schindler's List,* where a Nazi marks a
Jew for death because the man was a professor of literature and
history and therefore deemed "non-essential." The Jew incredu-
lously asks: "Non-essential? Since when are history and literature
non-essential?" And yet, with their preoccupation for "competing
in a global economy," many administrators take the Nazi's position with respect to the role of the humanities in education and in
life.

How this comes about is all too understandable. As soon as we
set foot in the wilderness of consumerism, the voice of the
Tempter whispers in our ear: "Bow down to me, and I shall give
you the science and the skills, the technical know-how and the
political outlook, to plunder the world of its goods." Knowledge
is power, so the pitch goes. Education is the key to success, the
passport to the future, the doorway to all that is pleasing to the
eye. Where educators perhaps once probed the depths of a question, salesmen now sit and plan their ad campaigns, always with
an eye toward the politically expedient, if not toward the politically correct. We have held the serpent to our breast for so long
that the temptation has assumed the appearance of wisdom. How
often do we hear, for example, the boast that the institution operates like a business and that the students are our customers? But
a customer is, by definition, a means to an end, a means to profit,
whereas our students are presumably the end of education itself,
the ones who are supposed to "profit" from the educational
endeavor.

Often I have heard college recruiters declare, "With us, students are Number One!" But this usually means that the students
are the first ones we exploit. The merchants have invaded the
Temple, where they peddle a mentality ruled by the dative case of

"to me" and "for me." Here, as in every marketplace, image is everything. And so education is smothered by what Kierkegaard calls "the despair of the immediate man." "For the immediate man," he says, "does not recognize his self, he recognizes himself only by his dress, . . . he recognizes that he has a self only by externals. There is no more ludicrous confusion, for a self is just infinitely different from externals" (1968, p. 187). To the extent that education is concerned with the soul, it also is just infinitely different from externals.

Among these merchants are not only the administrators of higher education but many of us who are members of the faculty in the humanities departments themselves. There, too, dollars eclipse all sense and sensibility, grantsmanship eats away at scholarship, and classroom numbers supersede classroom learning. Again, this is not to say that faculty and department heads need give no thought to budgets or that we should be indifferent to enrollments. However, it does mean that when we design our curricula, our concern should be focused more on filling minds with insight than on filling rooms with bodies. It means that we must offer our students what is needful to the life of the soul (if we ourselves have not forgotten) rather than cater to what they, who are uneducated, claim they want. By treating students as consumers and education as a commodity, we become blind to the truth that the real end of education is to impart more *to* life, not to extract more *from* life. Too often we anticipate our "customer's" question of "What is it good for?" and fabricate ready answers that eliminate the infinitely more needful questions of why we live and die, of what we stand for and will not stand for. Only after *these* questions have been raised can we address with any wisdom the question of what it is good for.

Drawn into the maelstrom of utilitarian materialism, we struggle to justify the humanities by explaining how a few courses in art, literature, or foreign languages might enhance career opportunities in business, technology, or the professions. At the very least, I have heard it argued, training in these areas makes for good cocktail conversation, where, as we know, careers often are advanced. Here the immediate man assumes the dress of the cultivated man whose training in the humanities increases his powers of negotiation at the expense of his capacity for human relation. Thus we place our unsuspecting youth on the altar of mammon, like the little one in William Blake's "A Little Boy Lost":

> The weeping child could not be heard,
> The weeping parents wept in vain;
> They strip'd him to his little shirt,
> And bound him in an iron chain.
> And burn'd him in a holy place,
> Where many had been burn'd before:
> The weeping parents wept in vain.
> Are such things done on Albion's shore?

Deaf to the cry of life represented by the cries of parent and child, we become the "they" that Blake describes. When that happens, we pay homage to Moloch at the thresholds of our hallowed halls, where our consumers are themselves consumed.

However, the idols of consumerism are worshipped not only for the gold of which they are made but for the power that they promise. Here the role of the humanities in higher education becomes the indoctrination of the young into politically correct "thinking," which has more to do with manipulation than with meditation. Instead of the analytical quest and questioning that characterize thought, the power brokers who disguise themselves as educators spread the fixed formulae and ready answers of party lines and personal agendas. Already, argues Bruce Edwards:

> they have succeeded in transforming the campus into a reeducation camp for training students for their prescribed role as exiles in their own culture: schools for autism that drive young minds deeper into subjectivity and solipsistic, "private morals." (1990, p. 5)

This project begins with the deconstruction of all higher truth to which any human being might be accountable; accountability is anathema to this idolatry. Here every form of the absolute is abrogated, so that the self becomes its own form of the absolute, its own authority of a counterfeit accountability. This situation, as Allan Bloom explains, is largely the result of deconstructionism, which:

> is the last, predictable, stage in the suppression of reason and the denial of the possibility of truth in the name of philosophy. The interpreter's creative activity is more important than the text; there is no text, only interpretation. Thus the one thing most necessary for us, the knowledge of what these texts have to tell us, is turned over to the subjective, creative selves of these interpreters, who say that there is both no text and no reality to which the texts refer. (1987, p. 379)

With the deconstruction of all higher truth to which any human being might be accountable, the self becomes as God. Once every form of the absolute is thus abrogated, the accidents of what meets the eye — such as gender or color — are made absolute. We see that both political correctness and deconstructionism proceed from the premise that all texts arise from ulterior motives that are in one way or another self-interested.

For example, in his critique of deconstruction, John Ellis maintains that theoretical argument "must be above all a careful, patient, analytical process," and that it is "very much a communal process: there is no room for individual license, for claims of exemption from logical scrutiny, for appeals to an undefined unique logical status, for appeals to allow obscurity to stand unanalyzed, or for freedom to do as one wishes" (1989, pp. 158-59). All of these, Ellis demonstrates, characterize deconstruction. The undermining of the analytical center that makes critical inquiry possible is accomplished with the pseudo-intellectual proclamation that everything — including and especially academic endeavor — is political, that the viewpoint of one peculiarity is as sound as the viewpoint of any other, that no one alien to a particular group can grasp the outlook peculiar to that group, and that power, rather than truth, is the basis of all human relation.

Thus the political discourse surrounding the humanities takes on the very characteristics that George Orwell ascribes to political language in general. It "is designed," he argues, "to make lies sound truthful and . . . to give an appearance of solidity to pure wind" (1983, p. 144). Here word is severed from meaning, so that words that mean nothing come to justify everything. The thought that once terrified Dostoevsky — that nothing is true and everything is permitted — now fascinates those who view the humanities not as a place where the truth of a common humanity may be pursued but as an opportunity to advance self-interests. Therefore, few are shocked at Martin Heidegger's address to the students of Freiburg on 3 November 1933, when he declared, "The Führer himself and he alone is German reality and its law, today and henceforth" (see Fackenheim 1989, pp. 167-68). As David Hirsch has shown, "it is now clear that Heidegger's attraction to National Socialism and his extended membership in the Nazi party were consistent with, rather than aberrant to, his thinking" (1992, p. 255). Allan Bloom explains:

> It was no accident that Heidegger came forward just after Hitler's accession to power to address the university community in Freiburg as the new rector, and urged commitment to National Socialism. His argument was not without subtlety and its own special kind of irony, but in sum the *decision* to devote wholeheartedly the life of the mind to an emerging revelation of being, incarnated in a mass movement, was what Heidegger encouraged. (1987, p. 311)

Thus we have the man who is arguably the father of deconstruction.

But the Nazi connection and all its implications do not end with Heidegger. Among the most prominent heirs to Heidegger's thinking is Jacques Derrida, who has labored to excuse Paul de Man's Nazi activities between 1940 and 1942, arguing that there is no relation between word and deed, thought and reality — in short, that there is no human accountability to a transcendent truth (1988, p. 651). Why? Because the divine I-for-myself that distinguishes this narcissistic solipsism isolates the human being from the human community by undermining the basis of that community. "As he has grown more desperate in his attempts to defend anti-Semites, collaborators, and Nazis," Hirsch points out, "Derrida's attacks on those who take issue with him have grown more ad hominem and more frenzied" (1992, p. 273). And as these attacks grow more frenzied, the attitude of I-for-myself that distinguishes Derrida's indefensible defense increasingly erases all principles that might guide learning and teaching activities.

Why bring up Heidegger, Derrida, and de Man in a discussion of the role of the humanities in higher education? Because thinkers such as these have contributed much to the general war on meaning now being waged within the humanities. Because, as Norman Fruman argues:

> One of the most important consequences of the de Man crisis has been the demonstration that the central tenets and techniques of deconstruction have proven utterly useless in disclosing anything special about controversial texts in a real situation, as opposed to the abstractions deriving from this or that 'reading' of Rousseau or Nietzsche or whoever, where nothing of consequence is really at stake. (1992, p. 45)

Wherever something is really at stake — as it is in our concern with the role of the humanities in higher education — we confront a higher responsibility to a higher truth that is neither mine nor yours; rather, it reveals itself as a third presence by which we are both judged and to which we are both accountable. But this accountability, which is the living center and the being-for-the-other that engender the life of humanity, is precisely what is under attack by the deconstructionist political correctness that opposes egocentrism to logocentrism and material power to transcendent truth.

In this opposition we can see that the two major threats to the humanities and higher education have something in common. Both the marketing of consumer goods and the spread of politically correct propaganda are driven by a sense of a strictly material reality for the sake of a strictly material self-interest. Both are geared to the wielding of power and the leveling of values, rather

106

than to a search for truth. Therefore, both are inimical to the essence of the humanities and of all that is higher in higher education. Yes, a consumer-based economy *can* benefit the public interest in higher education. Yes, the deconstructionist challenge to truth and reason *can* bring about a renewed and needful examination of our thinking in the humanities. But these things can happen only if we keep careful sight of a higher truth and a deeper sanctity common to all humanity.

What Ought to Be the Role of the Humanities in Higher Education?

In order to respond to this question, let us first consider the essence of education as it ought to be conceived. Here it may be helpful to recall the Hebrew word for education, *chinuch,* which also means "consecration" and "dedication." Rabbi Kalonymus Kalman Shapira, the Rebbe of the Warsaw Ghetto, explains, "The root [of *chinuch*] *CH-N-CH* implies the initial entry of a person or an object into a trade or path that is his destiny. Thus we find the root *CH-N-CH* referring to the education of a child, the consecration of the altar in the holy temple, and the dedication of a house" (1991, p. 4).

To have a destiny is to have not just an aim but a *higher* aim, to which we are answerable and by which we are judged. The notion of a destiny implies a mission or a meaning to be fulfilled, a word to be offered or a deed to be performed at a certain place and time; it implies a stepping before the Countenance, which we behold not prior to but in the midst of an act of response. In this we discover that freedom is linked to destiny, that it lies not in doing whatever I want to do but in the realization of what I must do. It lies not in choosing good or evil but in the relation to the Good that has already chosen me. Indeed, the condition of already having been chosen is what makes all of our subsequent choices meaningful. "The attachment to the Good precedes the choosing of this Good," Emmanuel Levinas insists. "How, indeed to choose the Good? The Good is good precisely because it chooses you and grips you before you have had the time to raise your eyes to it" (1990*b*, p. 135).

This notion of the Good underlies the notion of *chinuch* as Rabbi Shapira understands it. It calls to mind Plato's insistence on a relation between what we study and a higher good that we must hold dear (see *Republic*, Plato 1961, p. 842). When applied to the role of the humanities in higher education, it tells us that we do not have the license to make the humanities into anything that suits us. Rather, study of the humanities must make us into something better, something more, something good.

Bearing in mind Rabbi Shapira's accent on the life of the human being, and not on material success or political advantage, we realize once more that the highest in higher education has its origins not in the Tree of Knowledge but in the Tree of Life. We see the lie of viewing reality "as a merely social construct," to use Edwards' expression, "and not as an external, public landscape where minds may meet and true statements about the world can be made" (1990, p. 7). Rabbi Shapira shows us that education is rooted in "life's attachment to life," which Henri Bergson views as the essence of ultimate concern (1954, p. 210). Education affirms this attachment — and with it an ultimate concern — through its attachment to the child. On such a view, of course, the child or youth is not the consumer whom we satisfy but the human soul that we sanctify. The summons to this sanctification, and not the difficulty of the subject matter, is what puts the *higher* into higher education. Levinas explains:

> Height introduces a sense into being. It is already lived across the experience of the human body. It leads human societies to raise up altars. It is not because men, through their bodies, have an experience of the vertical that the human is placed under the sign of height; because human being is ordained to height, the human body is placed in a space in which the high and the low are distinguished and the sky is discovered. (1987*a*, p. 100)

Because the student opens up to us the sacred placed in our care, he or she opens up the dimension of height in the process of teaching. And *chinuch* means "education" because it implies this height; education happens only where life matters, and life comes to matter only when the distinction between high and low is central to it.

The other connotations of the word *chinuch* — the consecration of the temple altar and the dedication of a home — also are applicable to a proper understanding of higher education. Indeed, in the allusion to the invasion of the merchants, I have already suggested an analogy between the Temple and the school. Taking the analogy a bit further, one sees that, as in the Temple, there is (or should be) in the school a process of drawing nigh unto the sacred that lies at the heart of the process of learning. In both places this drawing nigh is effected by means of the word, and one recalls that, according to the Hebrew tradition, study is a form of prayer. This movement toward the sacred may happen in any area of study, but it is especially characteristic of the humanities. Think of Aristotle, Plotinus, Augustine, Chaucer, Michelangelo, Cervantes, Milton, Goethe, Chekhov, Akhmatova — what rules the ultimate concern of these artists and thinkers, if not a concern for the holy, for the meaningful, for what there is to hold dear in life?

This concern is what makes these figures representatives of the humanities, despite the differences that distinguish them. And what would the humanities be without a concern for such figures? According to Jewish tradition, the windows of the two Temples were designed not to let light in but to allow light to emanate into the world. And so it is with these thinkers in their pursuit of life's sacred center, of the living center symbolized by the Temple, the center without which we have neither a common humanity nor a human community but only a hodgepodge of special interest groups vying for an advantage along the edge of the void. Even in the midst of the attack on logocentrism — that is, on the proposition that there is a higher truth at work in life — one finds, perhaps, a sense of urgency that betrays an aching for the center, for the origin of meaning and truth, for the light that constitutes the origin. Even at the heart of the deconstructionists' efforts to level all texts, all lifestyles, into a valueless sameness, there is, perhaps, a longing for something higher to love, a longing for the commandment to love, which Levinas identifies with God (1988, p. 176-77). "You think you're cursing Him," Elie Wiesel expresses it, "but your curse is praise; you think you're fighting Him, but all you do is open yourself to Him; you think you're crying out your hatred and rebellion, but all you're doing is telling Him how much you need His support" (1966, p. 33). A human being can not glorify the void without being engulfed by it. And the humanities cannot abandon the sacred without glorifying the void.

The act of consecration implied by *chinuch* stands in opposition to the void, for it stands in opposition to indifference; and the void is the void of indifference, where, in the words of Levinas, "the bottom has dropped out of everything, an atmospheric density, a plenitude of the void, or the murmur of silence" (1987*b*, p. 46). Edmond Jabès compares the landscape of indifference to the landscape of the desert, where "one becomes other: one becomes the one who knows the weight of the sky and the thirst of the earth; the one who has learned to take account of his own solitude. Far from excluding us, the desert envelops us" (1990, p. 16). However, under the weight of an indifferent sky and an enveloping desert, a human being cannot remain indifferent if he is to remain human. The human response to the wilderness of the desert is the establishment of a dwelling place that consecrates and is consecrated by a place of learning. For dwelling is possible only where learning transpires. This point brings us to the third meaning of *chinuch,* the one pertaining to the dedication of a home.

Here, too, there are ties to what ought to be the role of the humanities in higher education. As Jabès' image of the desert suggests, one way to express the fundamental problem of human being — which should be a fundamental concern of the humanities — is to say that it is the problem of homelessness, of creating a place to dwell. The search for the center that may provide the basis for a human community is a search for the origin, for the Good that summons us prior to all freedom of our own making. The Good, as Buber has said, "is the movement in the direction of home" (1965, p. 78). In an age when proclamations of "God is dead" and "nothing is true, everything permitted" have become almost axiomatic, when more people spend more time in the work place and marketplace than in the home, when feeling takes precedence over thought, and the accidents of nature such as gender and color are academic qualifications — in such an age the human condition is a condition of exile. As is often the case, what manifests itself as a form of political punishment or a social and economic failure is symptomatic of a deeper, existential malady.

Indeed, the journeys of an Odysseus or a Dante or a Faust are efforts to make a movement homeward in the light of a spiritual exile. Essential to dwelling in a home is the presence of a family, and we pay much lip service to the importance of the family. But very little is said about the law, the truth, and the meaning symbolized from ancient times by the father, about the love, compassion, and kindness symbolized by the mother, or about the hope, the aspiration, and the dearness of life symbolized by the child. From the *Oresteia* of Aeschylus to the novels of Balzac, from *King Lear* to *The Brothers Karamazov,* these key ingredients of home and family have been central to the texts of the humanities. The role of the home in the human community and the role of the humanities in higher education have one thing in common: the sanctification of human life through the endeavor to understand something more about why we live and die. Like the family that brings us into the world and lays us to rest, the humanities lead us along the way from our origin to our end.

Where does that path take us? Is it to be a wandering in the wilderness or a return to some kind of spiritual homeland? The role of the humanities in higher education is, among other things, to decide such questions concerning the exile and the kingdom. If the modern existentialists have done nothing else, they have at least made our exile manifest through such works as *Nausea* and *No Exit* by Jean-Paul Sartre or *The Stranger* and *The Plague* by

Albert Camus. What, indeed, can be more haunting, more terrifying, than Meursault's last words in Camus' novel: "For everything to be consummated, for me to feel less alone, I had only to wish that there be a large crowd of spectators the day of my execution and that they greet me with cries of hate" (1988, p.123).

Significantly, Meursault has very little in the way of any relation to his mother, to the origin and basis of life. In fact, he has very little relation to anyone. It happens, therefore, that he commits a murder almost by "accident" and with no remorse. In Meursault, we recognize the image of postmodern man, who is distinguished by his indifference to murder, from drive-by shootings to genocide, from Los Angeles to Tibet. Hence in Meursault's last words and all around us we see the condition of the castaway that Walker Percy, for example, describes when he writes:

> In his heart of hearts there is not a moment of his life when the castaway does not know that life on the island, being 'at home' on the island, is something of a charade. At that very moment when he should feel most at home on the island, when needs are satisfied, knowledge arrived at, family raised, business attended to, at that very moment when by every criterion of island at-homeness he should feel most at home, he feels most homeless. (1982, p. 143)

All the conventions conspire to make our fortress assume the furniture of a home, until the words of a Meursault awaken us from our slumber and open our eyes to the abyss that yawns at our feet. Suddenly what is most needful seems most impossible: a sense of belonging. In the realm of education this means a sense of *chinuch,* which is the capacity for consecrating a home where the family may gather in an affirmation of life's sacred center.

When in his *Confession* Tolstoy declares, "I could not live" (1983, p. 29), it is his way of saying, "I did not belong": The message in the bottle, the word from the other shore that would make dwelling possible by making it meaningful, would not come. Jabès articulates this condition well when he says, "I feel that I exist only outside of any belonging. The non-belonging is my very substance. Maybe I have nothing else to say but that painful contradiction: like everyone else, I aspire to a place, a dwelling-place, while being at that same time unable to accept what offers itself" (1990, p. 29). What is given, it seems, is never what is needful; the truth is something sought, not something found. The result of the continual miscarriage of this aspiration for a place to dwell, Jabès goes on to argue, is that "we all suffer from an absence of identity which we desperately try to fill. It is in this despair that identity really resides" (p. 67).

If, as Jabès claims, identity resides in this despair, it resides in the form of something absent, like the unoccupied chair in a classroom that we know *ought* to be occupied. It is this absence that leads us to ask, "Where is this person?" or, in the case at hand, "Where am I?" This absence of identity arises from the heart of a breach between word and meaning, between the truth sought and the situation encountered, between what we sense as the needful and the sham that passes itself off as the desirable. From the core of this rupture, the role of the humanities is to ask the question born of this absence, a question that always concerns our relation to the truth we seek. Truth, Jabès maintains, lies on the other side of this question, "on the other shore, behind the last horizon" (p. 59). And the place where truth resides is precisely the place that we call home. It perhaps does not matter whether any absolute truth exists or whether we know beforehand what we are after, we need the process more than we need the outcome; and we must doom ourselves before we set out.

Remember the exchange between Ivan and Alyosha in Dostoevsky's *The Brothers Karamazov*. "How am I to love life more than the meaning of it?" Ivan wants to know. "How can I love life if I do not know its meaning?" To which Alyosha answers: "You must love it even though you have yet to understand it. It's only by loving life that you can ever hope to understand it" (1980, p. 213). If Camus' assertion that suicide is the only "truly serious philosophical problem" is true (1955, p. 3), then the role of the humanities is to provide a response, if not a solution, to that problem. And so the humanities reply: choose life. For only then can we hope to see the *why* of our choosing.

Thus, regarding the matter of what the humanities are useful for, we find that the true response runs far deeper than the usual answers geared to successful careers, political power, and other forms of idol worship that further entrench us in a state of exile. The humanities are useful — if that is still the right word — for posing the questions and the quest that sanctify life and thus enable the human being to dwell in a community that fosters life, rather than simply to survive a power struggle that inevitably ends in death. They are useful for approaching and addressing the sacred center that makes possible a human community that we may call "home." They are useful for engendering the embrace of the other human being that makes every other endeavor in life meaningful.

"You see," Dostoevsky once said, "I know that there is nothing higher than this thought of *embracing;* what will you, with your positivism, give me in the place of that?" (1974, p. 529). Why does he make such a statement? Because the embrace signifies the dearness and the depth of the other human being. It signifies the *significance* of the other, so that only through the act of embracing another do I take on significance of my own. In the movement of embrace we have the proximity that Levinas describes when he says, "Proximity is quite distinct from every other relationship, and has to be conceived as a responsibility for the other, it might be called humanity, or subjectivity" (1981, p. 46). And the humanities are useful for engendering this proximity and this humanity. They are useful for drawing nigh unto the human face, which, Levinas argues, forbids us to kill (1985, p. 86). In short, the humanities are useful for taking on a capacity to answer, "Here I am," to the first three questions put to humanity (which are actually a single question): Where are you? Where is your brother? And what have you done?

What ought to be the role of the humanities in higher education? To provide an alternative to the materialism and the nihilism that, in our despair, we come to adore. To return life to a relation to the center where home and school meet. To nurture the embrace and realize the prohibition that make life sacred.

The Stake in the Issue

By now it should not be too difficult to respond to the question of what is at stake in our concern with the humanities or of why we raise these issues. The stake in the issue is the very life of humanity and the human being, the life not only of a community of learning but of the community as such. Let us consider, then, the importance of raising the issue of the humanities' role in education, as well as the reasons for having thus described what it ought to be.

From merely a casual glance at the matter, one realizes that what is at stake in this discussion is the life and death of the young souls who are placed in our care. But it is not only *their* life and death. For in each soul we are entrusted with many souls, with lives that go beyond the scope of our comprehension. Just as the twelve hundred Jews on Schindler's list now number nearly seven thousand — just as those lives are lived in the memory of countless lives lost — so do we encounter innumerable lives, past and present and future, each time we go into a classroom. In the consecration of a single life, as in its betrayal, we consecrate or betray a world. He who saves a single life, we are taught in the Mishnah, is regarded as though he had saved the entire world (*Sanhedrin* 4:5).

Often the young men and women whose gaze we meet are entrusted to us by mothers and fathers who were the first to gaze into their eyes — and who, from the depths of those eyes, caught a glimpse of the mystery of the Most Dear. No human being who has held an infant only seconds old can doubt the summons that calls to us from within and from beyond our embrace of the little one. Once we have gazed into that face, the face of creation itself is transformed. And so, in many cases, our students are sent to us by people who have labored for a generation so that their children

115

might come to us and hear what we have to say. "My treasure," as I have heard one father refer to his son.

What, then, shall we say to the sons and daughters of these people? Shall we tell them, as they take their first steps away from home and into the world, that nothing matters beyond the satisfaction of ego and appetite? Shall we say that anyone whose life is not a mimicry of their own is a matter of indifference? Shall we tell them that their own lives, therefore, are meaningless? They ask us for bread, and all too frequently we give them the stone of gross materialism; they extend their hand for a fish, and we offer them the serpent of a politically correct power struggle.

Nor are these young men and women as stupid as we may think. In their heart of hearts they see only too well that success alone, defined as it usually is by purchasing power, cannot nourish the soul; that the surface features of gender, color, and ethnic peculiarity cannot provide the basis for inner substance and meaning; and that existence cannot be sustained when the sleep of self-centered indifference is taken to be the highest good in life. They see this, but, unfortunately, they do not have the education to respond to it. All too often we do not offer them that education.

If they schedule their classes around soap operas, talk shows, and MTV, it is not because they are shallow; it is because we, their teachers, are shallow. It is because we have failed to engage them with the high drama, the urgent discourse, and the artistic expression that might open up for them the affirmation of a reality that they may choose over the unreality that abounds all around us. By "unreality" I have in mind a political system in which politicians cannot be trusted, an education system in which teachers are suspected of incompetence, and a moral system in which the good is determined by whatever feels good. We should be shocked, then, but not surprised that among people in their late teens the leading causes of death are either drug- and alcohol-related or suicide. Among African-American males in this age group, murder is the number-one killer; and it is nearly always at the hands of another young black male. In the case of the former we see the young opting for the Big Sleep in an age distinguished by a somnambulistic turning away from human suffering and outcry; in the latter we see the violence that arises when words are torn from meaning and there is nothing left to say. How long will it take for us to rise from our own sleep and hear their outcry above the drone of our complacency? How many of these young human beings have to die before we get the message?

The stake in addressing the role of the humanities in higher education is more closely tied to this question than it may seem at first glance. For the most part, the youngsters who fall prey to drugs, suicide, and murder are not kids who have failed to learn the lessons they are taught in the education system. On the contrary, they have learned the lessons of the value-free void only too well and have followed those lessons to their logical conclusions, into the void itself, where they collide with what Levinas calls the "there is." The "there is," as he describes it, "is the phenomenon of impersonal being. It is a noise returning after every negation of this noise. Neither nothingness nor being. . . . One cannot say of this 'there is' which persists that it is an event of being. One can neither say that it is nothingness, even though there is nothing. *Existence and Existents* tries to describe this horrible thing, and moreover describes it as horror and panic" (1985, pp. 48-49).

Yet in may quarters of academia this horror and panic have been transformed into a postmodern exhilaration and intoxication over the leveling of that vertical dimension of life from which the meaningful derives its meaning. But the dimension of height in higher education implies an authoritative standard, not just with respect to academics but also with respect to the virtues upon which a community may stand and a life may be affirmed. In a world where anything goes — the undermining of meaning, the deconstruction of truth, the desecration of the holy — all of it is ineluctably tied to the indifferent drone of empty words that result in the loss of life among our youth. For if anything goes, then murder goes. If anything goes, then guns are a legitimate means of settling a dispute. And so, according to an ABC News report aired on 20 January 1994, elementary and junior high school children are being murdered at the rate of twelve per day, often *in the schools themselves.*

Like most things in human life, this death in the midst of our schools is not without its meaning and its message. We who work in the schools, at all levels, are responsible for what transpires within them. If death is among the things that arise in our schools, it is because, in various and veiled ways, it is part of what we teach. Therefore the stake in addressing the role of the humanities in education is to determine whether there is anything inconsistent between what we teach and this death toll that continues rise among youth of all ages. In the contexts of what we have examined, the famous question raised by Levinas — "Do I not kill by being?" (1985, p. 210) — becomes: Do I not deprive another human being in my insistence on having more? Do I not oppress another human being by demanding my rights to the exclusion of his or hers? Do I not arrive at my self-esteem at the expense of my esteem for the other human being?

If we take these questions seriously, then we may find that the role of the humanities in higher education is not to increase earning power, political power, or the elusive "self-empowerment." If the humanities are to become what I have argued they ought to be, then they must become central to our ability to respond to the outcry of imperiled life. Thus, if we are to eliminate every inconsistency between what we teach and the projects of death, then we must stand for all that sanctifies life whenever we stand before our students. Otherwise we become accomplices to the killing. And where will this education and consecration of life, this *chinuch,* take place within our institutions, if it does not take place within the humanities?

Rabbi Kalonymus Kalman Shapira was not only the Rebbe of the Warsaw Ghetto, he was one of the teachers in the Ghetto, those who did their work under the threat of death and attended to children who, they knew, were marked for the flames of Treblinka. His example poses a decisive question for every one of us — not only the question of whether we could do the same but of whether we could express the point in doing it at all. For Rabbi

Shapira, the school was neither a business venture nor a success mill. Nor was it a depot for politically correct indoctrination. Indeed, *there is no inconsistency* between these views of the school and the mass murder carried out both in the Ghetto and beyond its walls. For Rabbi Shapira, the school represented the one place of sanctity, the only ray of light, in a world ruled by the darkness of material power, physical violence, and ethnic authority. Interestingly — but not coincidentally — the humanities formed the core of the curriculum in the Ghetto's schools: Jewish history, Hebrew language, the literature of holy texts, as well as other works. In the comfort of our classrooms and offices, of course, we are light years from the Warsaw Ghetto and must be very careful about any comparisons that we might make. Yes, light years away. . . .

But the universe is the same. What sanctifies life is the same. And the summons that rises up from the heart of the humanities, the summons to affirm the holiness of humanity, is the same. Quite unlike Rabbi Shapira, we do not have to answer from the very pit of the shadow of death; we do not have to answer when every affirmation of life is rendered either impossible or absurd or both. Ours is a much more comfortable situation. So, how shall we answer?

The Honors Student, the Professor, and the Program in Higher Education

In a system of higher education where traditional academic standards are assailed for being oppressive, patriarchal, and logo-centric, it is not surprising to find that honors programs often are attacked for being elitist or exclusive. The difficulty is not so much that universities do not want such programs, but rather that they do not want them to be *honors* programs in any serious sense of the word. Enrollments, for example, are often taken to be more important than curriculum and instruction. Or it happens that the demographics of the program are of a higher concern than the usual academic standards. I heard one dean argue, for instance, that some "traditional" students (meaning Caucasians) who are academically qualified should be refused a place in the honors program, so that others (meaning racial minorities) can partici-pate, despite the possible lack of academic qualification. It looks better, is the argument I have heard. Just as an honors lounge and living space, new computers, and newsletters look better. And things that look better will attract more honors students.

Thus in an age when consumerism rules consciousness and the marketplace determines direction — when the politics of race and gender shape the landscape of knowledge and scholarship — we are more concerned with presenting the politically correct surface to the public, whose dollars we adore, than with present-ing the proper education to the students placed in our care.

The concern with such surface features as enrollments or demographics often becomes a concern for image at the expense of essence. Or perhaps better stated: It leads to a confused identification of image with essence. Yet, paradoxically, the identification of image with essence is just what creates a divorce of image from essence, making one not only different from but opposed to the other. The external and the internal, the immediate and the ultimate, do not mix. The more we are known by our possessions or social status — the more we are defined by our gender or skin color — the more we are in conflict with the dimension of depth that truly determines our essence as human beings.

However, if our interest lies with the truth that is at the center of inner life and higher education, then the concern that guides us is an ultimate concern that must be conveyed through immediate concerns. In this way surface is transformed from "window dressing" into symbol, which, in the words of Karl Jaspers, "makes not only clear but *real* what would otherwise be like nothing" (1959, p. 40). Gathered into the symbol, image need not be opposed to or confused with essence; rather, it becomes a vehicle or an expression of essence, so that form and substance are interconnected without being reduced to the same thing.

The principle that Mikhail Bakhtin applies to the study of texts, then, might equally apply to an examination of university honors programs in higher education. Words play a large role in the formation of such programs, and any analysis of them entails a certain reading of them. "The study of verbal art," Bakhtin argues, "can and must overcome the divorce between an abstract 'formal' approach and an equally abstract 'ideological' approach" (1981, p. 259). When we are dealing with students, we are not dealing with abstractions. Rather, we are dealing with people who seek some deeper understanding of their lives through a deeper penetration into the academic disciplines. For this they turn to people who, like it or not, are teachers all the time, not just during the fifty minutes of class time.

Therefore we would do well to follow the advice that Father Zossima gives to his monks in Dostoevsky's *The Brothers Karamazov*:

Every day and every hour walk around yourself and watch yourself, and see that your image is a seemly one. You pass by a little child, you pass by, spiteful, with ugly words, with an angry heart; you may not have noticed the child, but he has seen you, and your image, unseemly and ignoble, may remain in his defenseless heart. You don't know it, but you may have sown an evil seed in him and it may grow, and all because. . . you did not foster in yourself a careful, actively benevolent love. (1980, p. 295)

In the case of the honors program, the image may not be ignoble, but it can certainly be shallow; and most honors students will sooner or later see through something that is all surface. They are good readers. More important, one will note that Dostoevsky underscores not only a seemly image and a loving essence but also the urgency of the relation between the two. One is tied to the other, each is shaped by the other, so that the soul is revealed in the face, and the face takes on the expression of the soul. Both harbor a testimony that places us in a position of responsibility for those whom we encounter.

From this interrelation of image and essence are sown the seeds that determine the ground we stand on and the path we follow. If it should occur to someone that Dostoevsky spoke of human beings, while we are speaking of honors education, it may be recalled that an honors program also has a personality or a soul of its own. It is constituted by the combination of those human beings, the students and the faculty, who belong to the program, as well as by those principles that rule the program. The men and women who make up the program, as well as its courses and requirements, constitute its face and impart to it a certain complexion. Here lies the link between the form and the substance of a program in honors education. But taking the Dostoevskian analogy further, we ask: What does honors education have to do with fostering a "careful, actively benevolent love?"

The love of which Dostoevsky speaks is an embrace of the highest and the dearest in life, of what is beyond the weights and measures of marketplace numbers, ethnic demographics, and test scores. Honors education, in its image and essence, should be steeped in just such an embrace, one that links not only form to substance but life to learning. To the extent that an honors program is distinguished by such an embrace, those who give it a face and soul meet their responsibility to their community. To the extent that such an embrace is absent from the program, those whose lives are entrusted to it — indeed, the entire community — are betrayed. From this embrace or betrayal are sown the seeds that decide life and death.

Thus the honors program is not simply one among a variety of college or university programs. It has a definitive effect on the nature of higher education. To be in an honors program is to be in a position of having to answer for what is *higher* in higher education, not merely for what is more advanced. The student who enters the program becomes a witness to the substance of learning. The professor who stands before an honors class stands for the stake in teaching. And the program that undertakes the honors endeavor testifies to the significance of education — if it is truly an *honors* program.

Learning: The Honors Student

It must be said at the outset that we are proceeding from a premise that takes the honors student to be not one of the elite but one of the exemplary. Regarded as one of the elite, the honors student is not only distinguished from his or her classmates but is placed at a distance from them. On the other hand, viewed as one of the exemplary, the honors student is not placed at a distance from other students but is drawn closer to them as a paradigm in their midst. We make this distinction between the elite and the exemplary in order to accentuate not just the outcome of learning but the learning *process,* which tends to be occluded by an elitist outlook. This distinction also is made in order to emphasize responsibility over privilege, a task to be performed over a goal already achieved.

Although he takes the elitist approach, Howard Davis appears to be taking a position similar to ours, when he insists that the "elite" students "brought together in an honors program have a special responsibility to serve the values that provide the stability and the rules necessary for freedom and democracy to flourish" (1989, p. 22). And John Osborne may seem to be assuming the stance we have taken, when he maintains that "honors is elitist in that it strives to help our most intelligent and motivated students to realize the great cultural possibilities to which they might not otherwise aspire" (1989, p. 29). However, both of these views place the student outside of the program and lose sight of what transpires *within* the honors student's learning process. The aspiration to democratic values or to cultural possibilities is empty unless it is grounded in an ongoing aspiration to the truth from which such values and possibilities are derived.

As an exemplary student, rather than an elite student, the honors student is one who might come a bit closer to becoming what other students aspire to become *as students*. In this view, the honors student is an example to whom others may turn not only to see how to study but to understand something of what study itself is all about, its essence. Thus the honors student establishes a link between the image and essence of learning through an exemplary relation to others. And so we ask: What does learning entail? What, indeed, is the nature of study as it is exemplified by the honors student?

In a speech delivered at the 20th Annual Scholars' Conference on 4 March 1990, Elie Wiesel made a comment that may help us to address these questions. It came in his response to the question of how he, as a survivor of the Holocaust, deals with the problem of continuing with life. After all, many have taken their own lives, among them such prominent figures as Tadeusz Borowski, Paul Celan, Jean Amery, Primo Levi, and Jerzy Kosinski, to name only a few. Wiesel replied that in his case it was not family or home that enabled him to endure, since these had been murdered and obliterated; nor was it his religion, since that had been seriously challenged. Rather, he said, the thing that kept him alive was a love for study.

If study can sustain a life, then it must have as its basis an ultimate concern or spiritual commitment that runs much deeper than mere curiosity. In a word, it must have a metaphysical aspect. "Man engages in metaphysics," José Ortega y Gasset expresses it, "when he seeks a basic orientation in his situation" (1969, p. 26), an orientation from which he finds his way not to the student union or the registrar's office but into the heart of life. In the case of Wiesel, this movement toward life is rooted in the fact that in the tradition of the People of the Book, study is a form of prayer, hence the rabbinic saying: When I pray I speak to God; when I study God speaks to me. God speaks to me from the depths of a question. For at the center of the Hebrew word for "question," *she'elah,* is the *aleph-lamed,* the *el,* that signifies God.

Regarded as a process of listening, study is not the accumulation of data or the memorization of facts but a dialogue with truth sustained by a questioning in which the student engages not only his subject matter but his own soul and the origin of the soul. The school or the program of study in which the student is enrolled is no longer a training center but a transcendent center. Wiesel himself exemplifies this attitude toward school and study when he writes, "If the school is a temple, then the library is its sanctuary. In the classroom you teach, you learn, you argue; in the library you remain quiet. You read alone; you listen alone. And all of a sudden you discover that you are not alone" (1990, p. 38). All of a sudden one discovers that what he or she is trying to penetrate is penetrating him- or herself.

This discovery is indeed an astounding one: A thought from another mind, from a distant place and time, has found its way into your mind. And this thought is laden with a legion of voices. Who is there with you? Those whose voices you seek and who, in turn, seek what you seek. "You hear my words," said the 14th-century Sufi Qandahari. "Hear, too, that there are words other than mine. These are not meant for hearing with the physical ear. . . . You are here to learn, not to collect historical information" (Shah 1968, pp. 166-67). "To learn" means establishing a connection between the Tree of Knowledge and the Tree of Life, between human knowing and human being. Information is faceless, whereas learning entails stepping before a countenance.

This religious discourse surrounding the link between life and learning does not have to be stretched very far to develop a connection with the honors student. Study may keep a man alive because study is a process of seeking a relation to the ground of life, of rejoining life with life; and this lends a religious element to learning, at least in Henri Bergson's sense of the term. Religion, he says, is "that element which is called upon to make good any deficiency of attachment to life" (1954, p. 210). The student who takes up any higher learning engages in a struggle to regain an attachment to life that arises with a cry of "I do not know." This not knowing is not only an ignorance of *how* or *what* but of *why*. The honors student takes education into the realm of the higher not merely by pursuing an advanced level of learning but by addressing the point in learning that is tied to the point in living: The process of learning is a participation in the process of creation. "Thus understanding fills out the text," says Bakhtin. "It is active and takes on a creative character. Creative understanding continues the creation; it multiplies the creative wealth of humanity" (1979, p. 346).

Viewed as a participation in the creation, the process of learning transcends the time of learning. As Wiesel states it, "the Talmud represents a possibility of transcending the present and extending its boundaries. We repeat an ancient discussion and we become its participants; we study the interpretation of old laws and customs, and they commit us anew. We recall what was said two thousand years ago, and we gain the impression that every word, every sentence, every question, and every answer were meant for us" (1991, p. 314). And the word Talmud means "learning." The process of learning exemplified by the Talmud is without end, as Wiesel points out: "Rav Ashi concluded the editing of the Babylonian Talmud but refrained from sealing it, and he did so on purpose: to allow us to continue" (1991, p. 314).

The nature of the learning process also is exemplified by the honors student. While learning may arise from an existing disorientation, from an "I do not know," its open-endedness orients us toward the yet-to-be, toward the invisible. And so once again we meet with metaphysics. As an exemplary student, the honors student imparts a metaphysical aspect to learning precisely because he or she has something yet to learn. Far from "knowing it all," the honors student is more profoundly lost than the average student, and this condition is what situates the honors student more firmly, more substantially, between his classroom and his living room. There, in this precarious "between" space, the essence of life and of learning is decided.

The religious or metaphysical dimension of learning invoked by Wiesel and Ortega y Gasset is precisely what instills learning with an essence. The essence of learning and the essence of the student *as student* are of a piece. And, as Ortega y Gasset suggests, that essence is initially sensed in the feeling of being lost: "To feel oneself lost! Did you ever consider what those words mean in themselves? Without going beyond them, to feel oneself lost implies first the sensation of feeling oneself — that is, meeting oneself, finding oneself" (1969, p. 31). The urgency that characterizes the honors student's learning process arises from a quest to understand something not only about the world but about oneself in relation to the world. The truth of the world and the truth of the soul are interwoven; deciding something about art, history, or physics, we decide something about ourselves. "The act of knowledge," the 14th-century philosopher Gersonides expresses it, "the object of knowledge, and the knower are all identical" (1984, vol. 1, p. 180). When this interrelation is at work, learning goes far beyond an effort to satisfy some head-scratching curiosity or the drive for a successful career or even the longing for social and political power. When the external world and the internal life are involved with one another, learning takes on a certain redemptive aspect by instilling the soul with life.

No longer, then, does the student seek merely to acquire the skills and the know-how that will enable him to make a living.

Having collided with a fundamentally lost condition — a lost self or soul — he or she sets out to make a life, to regain a life or an essence that perhaps had never been part of the student's consciousness. And so the quest takes the student elsewhere, beyond the confines of the ego, which is the object of misguided self-centeredness and self-esteem. Consciousness, indeed, is consciousness of something or someone outside of oneself. "Consciousness," in the words of Emmanuel Levinas, "is the urgency of a destination leading to the other person and not an eternal return to the self" (1990*b*, p. 48). Thus for the honors student, as an exemplary student, learning is not a matter of accumulating information or even of "self-actualization" but of creating a relation to another; it is distinguished not by soaking up knowledge but by offering up oneself.

This is an act that no one else can perform for the student. That is why Rabbi Kalonymus Kalman Shapira, the Rebbe of the Warsaw Ghetto, insists that the most important thing to impart to the student is that "he must know that he himself is his own most basic and important educator" (1991, p. 15). For he himself is the origin of the relation and the offering to another that nurtures life. Therefore, if it is knowledge he seeks, it is a knowledge, as Levinas puts it, "in which its messenger is simultaneously the very message" (1990*b*., p. 48). Moreover, the creation of a relation through an offering up of the self lies in the development of responsibility — that is, of "response ability," or a capacity for response. As a matter of urgency for the life of the soul, learning cannot occur apart from an act of response, for this is the act that engenders presence and therefore relation in life. To attend is to listen, and to be present is to have a voice. Learning is just this sort of voice training, so that learning is the means by which the soul might be filled with life. And with truth.

For the honors student, "truth," as Kierkegaard expresses it, "consists not in knowing the truth but in being the truth" (1944*b*, p. 201). What is learning but a process through which the soul continually endeavors to become the truth and thereby to take on reality: the messenger is the message. The Russian thinker Pavel

Florensky notes in this connection that the

> Russian word for "truth" [*istina*] is linguistically tied to
> the verb "to be" [est] (*istina — estina*). Thus, in keeping
> with the Russian understanding of it, "truth" entails in itself
> a concept of absolute reality. Truth is "the real."(1970, p. 15)

The reality or the being of the student is definitively linked to
the truth he pursues. And the honor of the honors student lies in
this linkage. For honor is tied not to laurels or accolades but to
honesty and integrity, which in turn are tied to being truthful. The
honors student is truthful, full of a truth manifested in the form of
the pursuit of truth. Therein lies his or her essence as a student.

Rather than simplify or clarify anything, it may seem at first
glance that this view of the student and of learning complicates our
notion of teaching. If the student's learning entails a return to life,
a responsibility to and for a truth that belongs to the essence of the
soul, then how are we to conceive of teaching? Given this approach
to learning, teaching cannot be viewed as drill, instruction, training, or any other activity commonly associated with teaching. In
fact, teaching is not an activity at all but an event, the other side of
the encounter that takes place when learning happens.

Teaching: The Honors Professor

Just as we have viewed learning in terms of process, so shall
we view teaching. This accent on process focuses our attention
not just on the poles of the student-teacher relation but on the ten-
sion and the movement between the poles. It places both learning
and teaching in a context of encounter or of dialogue. Thus it situates teacher and student in the present.

In this connection the Brazilian educator Paulo Freire argues
that the educational process "is an act of knowing in which the
learner assumes the role of knowing subject in dialogue with the
educator, . . . a process through which men. . . begin to assert. . .
the right of self-expression and world-expression, of creating and
re-creating, of deciding and choosing and ultimately participating

in society's historical process" (1970, pp. 29-30). Freire's words teem with all the exigency of a sense of duty, and the progressive mood of his verbs places this duty before us. We see that, as a teacher, he has heard a commandment: The attention he would give to his students derives from having heard an order from elsewhere. Answering that order, he engages his student in dialogue.

Freire's words confirm Franz Rosenzweig's insight that "the commandment is the first content to drop into this attentive hearing" (1972, p. 176). The teacher is he who knows what must be done. The small honors classes that are designed to promote discussion also impose a demand for dialogue on the honors professor. The professor is summoned to be not just a "professional" (a term some in higher education use to avoid their humanity) but also a human being. When teaching takes place within a context of dialogical encounter, the professor must teach not just from texts, charts, or overhead projections but from the heart and soul of his very life. The messenger must become the message.

This presence of the teacher as a human being in the midst of the teaching situation is what makes it a *living* situation. This presence is what lends the face-to-face encounter a personality and a face of its own. The encounter assumes a face when the teacher becomes not just the bearer but the transmitter of the word, in such a way that his life instills his words with meaning.

For the life of the human being constitutes the life of the word, and "the life of the word," as Bakhtin has said, "is contained in its transfer from one mouth to another, from one context to another" (1984, p. 202). This shifting of contexts is what comprises the teaching context, since contexts shift with every act of listening and response. The term *context,* moreover, is to be taken literally, in that the teacher and the student are gathered together before a text in order to generate a text in an act of response. In this way the word of a text — regarded as both book and situation, as written word and spoken word — takes on a life and attaches itself to life.

"For a word," Rosenzweig reminds us, "does not remain its speaker's possession; he to whom it is addressed, he who hears it, or acquires it by chance — they all get a share of it; the word's fate, while in their possession, is more fate-ful than what its original speaker experienced when first uttering it" (1955, p. 73). Rosenzweig's remark may give us a deeper sense of the import of Freire's allusion to historical process, for his use of "fate-ful" is intended to invoke the meaningful: As a word conveys meaning, so it instills life with meaning and meaning with life in its transfer from mouth to mouth.

Like "fate," meaning suggests direction; and direction points toward a task. As one who must establish a presence through an act of response, the primary task of the honors professor is not to provide fixed formulas and ready answers, which only eclipse the voice. Rather, his or her main task is to summon the voice of the student through a response to the student, so that the aim is not to have the last word but to sustain the meeting of word with word. The aim, stated differently, is to introduce time, or a certain history, to the process of teaching and learning — a history of meaning that opens up the pursuit of a future. Therefore, Adin Steinsaltz explains:

> One of the great talmudic commentators, the Maharsha, often ended his commentaries with the word *vedok* (continue to examine the matter). This exhortation is an explicit admission that the subject has not been exhausted and that there is still room for additions and arguments on the question. (1976, p. 273).

So might the honors professor end every class session with this summons to examine the matter further.

So might the honors professor begin every class. Indeed, tradition has it that the first-century rabbi, Rabban Gamaliel, would enter his school and begin his class with a single word: Ask! (Finkelstein 1981, p. 112). Once again we are reminded of the presence of the *el* in the midst of the *she'elah*. At the heart of the question there abides a voice, whose summons the professor must convey. It is the voice that called Freire to the dialogue he describes above. One who is adept at conveying such a summons to his students is versed not only in speech and explanation but also is a highly attentive listener who, with all the urgency of ultimate concern, attends to the call that comes both from the student and from beyond him — from his or her question. The imperative, "Ask!" harbors the declarative, "I am listening." Hence, the talmudic sage Ben Zoma once asserted, "he is wise who learns from all people" (*Avot* 4:1).

Just so, the teacher is wise who learns from all students; the teacher teaches by becoming a student. Thus exemplifying the responsibility for learning that he would engender, the honors professor both calls upon the student and is himself called upon. Here, too, the notion of the elite is overtaken by the notion of the exemplary, in such a way that the honors professor becomes a paradigm not only of the teacher but of the student. Not just in the classroom but, again, in his or her way of life — in study, scholarship, and classroom encounter, at home and on the street — the honors professor demonstrates what it means to pursue the truth, as well as the fact that the truth is worth pursuing, that, indeed, it insists upon being pursued. "All revelation is a calling and a mission," Martin Buber maintains (1970, p. 164), and so it is with the honors professor. He is the student who has reached the point in a pursuit of truth from which he cannot help but teach, if he is to pursue it further. To be sure, we learn by teaching; we proceed by explaining; we understand by asking.

Therefore, the honors professor is the opposite of the "expert." As with the rabbinic teachers of old, the highest compliment one can pay to the honors professor is to say that he or she is a *talmid chakham,* a wise student.

This is why the Talmud places such emphasis both on learning and on teaching, recognizing that each is an aspect of a single event. Teaching is part of learning, and to receive the Torah is to impart the Torah (see *Avot* 4:5), in word and in deed. To study the Torah is to be *commanded* to transmit it and in that transmission to regenerate life. That "each person must be careful to seek new insights in the Torah," the 18th-century scholar Rabbi Yaakov Culi notes, is "included in the commandment 'be fruitful and multiply'" (1977, p. 129). New insights are obtained only dialogically, between two who are seeking those insights. With each new insight comes a new commandment, one that is not merely a new rule to follow but a new portal through which the meaningful and the dear may enter into life and thereby increase its depth.

Encountering once more the notion of commandment, we come to the issue of ability. Rosenzweig's thinking proves helpful: "Ability means: not to be able to do otherwise — to be obliged to act" (1955, p. 90). Inasmuch as being a teacher implies having a certain ability, to be a teacher is to be obliged. To be a teacher, therefore, is to be chosen prior to making any other choices. This is what makes it an honor to teach honors students. Underlying the honor is not just a recognition of ability but also the affirmation of obligation. All honors that are truly an honor are humbling. The honors professor is humbled by the charge placed in his care and by his or her having been chosen for such a task. There is nothing inherent in a given subject or course that would distinguish it as "honors" in contrast to the standard fare. Rather, it is the spirit in which the course is taught — the image and the essence of the teaching endeavor — that places it into the category of honors.

While the student's task in the learning process is to regenerate a relation of life to life, the professor is the one who attests to the dearness and the depth of the bond between one human being and another. There is no other way to establish a relation with the truth that the professor would transmit, for "the direct relation with the true," says Levinas, "can only be the relation with a person, with another" (1990*b*, p. 47). This means that the true is the ethical. Because the relation with the true entails a certain contact with another person, the teaching relation is essentially an ethical relation. Indeed, it is the ethical relation *par excellence.* If learning has its metaphysical aspect, teaching has its ethical aspect, so that both meet in the bond between honors student and honors professor. Because honors teaching, like honors learning, is a matter of creating a certain link with another, both transpire in a space *between* the honors student and the honors professor, as the concept of linkage implies. Because teaching is an encounter that takes place between teacher and student, the truth that constitutes each lies outside of both. The truth is not in your head but is between heads and hearts and souls. That is what makes teaching an ethical matter, and one of great urgency. We can decide whether to purse it or betray it, but we cannot decide whether it is important.

Therefore, the thing conveyed to the student by the honors professor is not so much a particular body of knowledge as a certain urgency about the search, an urgency that lies in an ethical accountability to and for the truth sought. From the standpoint of the professor, the student announces that urgency. In the words of Levinas, "The privilege of the Other in relation to the I — or moral consciousness — is the very opening to exteriority, which is also an opening to Highness" (1990*a*, p. 294). If there is something "higher" about the honors program in higher education, it lies in this higher responsibility, which unfolds in the ethical, dialogical encounter between teacher and student. Where the embrace of this higher responsibility is absent, there can be no higher learning and no higher teaching, but merely a vocational training that goes under the guise of "higher" education.

Hence we discover that the religious dimension of the learning process has its counterpart in the teaching endeavor. In its metaphysical aspect, the religious dimension entails a relation to the source of life and the ground of meaning. In its ethical aspect it entails a relation to the other human being. When both of these aspects are at work, a program happens. Thus we come to a final, most crucial question about the image and essence of higher education as it is revealed in the honors program. What does this higher, essential responsibility that distinguishes honors learning and teaching reveal about higher education?

Higher Education: The Honors Program

As with the honors student and the honors professor, I shall approach the honors program in terms of the exemplary rather than in terms of the elite. The honors program is the one program that should exemplify what any program in higher education is all about. In order to determine what is *higher* in higher education as it is represented by the honors program, we should begin with the phenomenon of education itself, that is, with the question of what it means to be educated.

Plato says it as well as anyone: "The rightly educated prove what we mean by good, and no aspect of education is to be disparaged; it is the highest blessing bestowed on mankind" (*Laws*, 1961, p. 1243). These words are as staggering in their profundity as they are in their implications. Recalling the Latin origin of the word *educate,* which is *educere,* we are reminded that to educate is to "lead forth." Lead forth to where? To the good, as Plato implies. If education is the highest blessing bestowed on mankind, it is because education is an avenue through which the good becomes part of the life of humanity. In the good we discover the intersection of the metaphysics and the ethics that have been invoked in our discussion of the honors student and the honors professor. If the aim of the honors program is to see to it that students are rightly educated, then the aim of the honors program is to reveal the good through the educational endeavor as it unfolds through a certain relation to the student.

Moreover, the aim of the program is the origin of the program. Says Levinas:

> The goodness of the Good — the Good which never sleeps or nods — inclines the movement it calls forth, to turn it from the Good and orient it toward the other, and only thus toward the Good. Here is an obliqueness that goes higher than straightforwardness. The desirable is intangible and separates itself from the relationship with desire which it calls for, through this separation or holiness it remains a third person, the *he* in the depth of the you. He is good in just this eminent sense; He does not fill me up with goods, but compels me to goodness, which is better than goods received. (1987*a*, p. 165)

Linked to the holy, the goodness of the good made manifest in the rightly educated person far transcends the power and goods tied to politics and consumerism. For this goodness is the goodness of the truth, which is inextricably interwoven with the sanctity of the human being.

Thus oriented toward the other — that is, toward the student and, through the other toward the good, the educational endeavor is the opposite of the business enterprise or political agenda. The school is comparable to the temple, as Wiesel suggests in his comment on the library, insofar as it signifies a sacred good in the sanctification of the human being. This signification is what makes higher education higher. And, like a sign within a sign, the honors program within the institution of higher education signifies the sanctity of this higher endeavor.

How does the honors program do this? I would contend that it is through its exemplary treatment of its students, which lies not just in the individual attention paid to a "customer" or in the "sensitivity" shown to a member of an ethnic culture. Rather, it lies in the one-to-one, face-to-face relation to a human being. In the face are gathered the image and the essence of the honors program. The face announces the responsibility that the program must meet and the summons that it must answer. Levinas explains:

> The epiphany of a face is a *visitation*. Whereas a phenomenon is already, in whatever respect, an image, a captive manifestation of its plastic and mute form, the epiphany of a face is alive. . . . The nudity of a face is a bareness without any cultural ornament, an absolution, a detachment from its form in the midst of the production of its form. A *face* enters into our world from an absolutely foreign sphere, that is, precisely from an absolute. (1987a, pp. 95-96)

Curriculum? Yes. Requirements? Of course. But these are the mute, inanimate forms into which the face of the human being, of student and teacher, breathes life. What is needful in the honors program, then, is not presenting a face to the public but allowing a face to enter into the program. For this is where the absolute — that is, the sacred, the true, and the good — enter into the program. This is where meaning enters into the program. The sphere of meaning is "foreign," to use Levinas' term, because it is infinite; it is the ever-sought-after that abides along the ever-expanding horizon of inquiry. The honors program exemplifies the essence of higher education to the extent that it is continually approaching this horizon. Its aim is not to complete an education but to reveal the open-endedness of an education that ascends higher and higher.

As an ongoing quest for what is higher in higher education, honors education entails a process of becoming that is essential to spiritual life. Remember Bakhtin's warning: *To cease becoming means spiritual death.* (1979, p. 109). Viewed in terms of a struggle for spiritual life against spiritual death, the honors program embodies the image and essence of "education" much as it is expressed by the corresponding Hebrew term. For the Hebrew word *chinukh* means not only "education" but also "consecration." If education is a process of coming to life, then it is a process of "making sacred," of sanctifying life by deeming it worth nurturing. The thing that makes teaching and learning into education, and not mere training, is this consecration, which determines the truth of the educational encounter and the honor of the honors program.

Recalling what was said about education's open-endedness, we see that this sanctification of life is, among other things, a process of transforming a dead past into a living tradition. A tradition is living to the extent that it is transmitted. As it is transmitted, it unveils a future. The word *future* means that life matters. "The other is the future," Levinas expresses this idea. "The very relationship with the other is the relationship with the future" (1987*b*, p. 77). Through the other, through *this human being*, the sacred manifests itself; and where life has sanctity it has a future. If the endeavor of the honors program entails a consecration of life, it includes the opening up of a future — for the student, for the professor, and for the program.

Because "the other is the future," the time of the honors program exceeds the program itself. It is the passage of the student's time beyond those confines that define him as a student, "the passage of the time of the other," as Levinas states it. He asks: "Should what makes such a passage possible be called *eternity*?" (1987*u*, p. 92). The question is rhetorical. If the honor of the honors program is enduring, it is because the program harbors a trace of the eternal as revealed in an ongoing responsibility to and for human life and the origin of that life. And that responsibility manifests itself in dialogue.

"The dialectic of time," writes Levinas, "is the very dialectic of the relationship with the other, that is, a dialogue" (1978, p. 93). In the *dialectic* of time we catch a glimpse of eternity as a presence that operates both outside and with time. This notion of time and eternity is not as esoteric as it may seem. It lies at the heart of the distinction between the exemplary and the elite. For the elite, time comes to a halt; that is to say, elite time is the time of the already achieved, of the already said, which Bakhtin describes as "the dead flesh of meaning" (1979, p. 117) — dead because the life of meaning requires a movement that is alien to the already achieved.

That movement is toward the other person. Again, for the honors program this means serving as an example to other students, teachers, and programs and thereby relinquishing privilege for responsibility. If I am to be an example for the other, then my time is for the other, the time I have is the time I give, and this is how we are to understand Levinas' assertion that the other is the future. This is how we are to understand his insistence that "responsibility for the other signifies an original and concrete temporality" (1987*b*, p. 104). As for eternity, it finds its way into the program through the responsibility that goes with setting yet a better example. Responsibility means that nothing is settled; responsibility is never at an end. On the contrary, it grows as it is met; in the words of Levinas, "The debt increases in the measure that it is paid" (1981, p. 12).

Each example set, each act of response, increases the capacity for response, so that we no sooner respond than we have held something back, something more that we must offer. As the voice of the highest in educational concerns, the honors program is

139

responsible for all other educational programs in the college or university community, responsible for education as such. Understood in terms of the exemplary, the honors student, professor, and program must forever become better and therefore confront ever increasing depths of responsibility; viewed in terms of the elite, they are already better and therefore enjoy a certain privilege. If the honors program is better, it is not merely because it has higher standards, better students, or more accomplished professors. No, if it is "better" in some sense, it is because the honors program cannot settle for what it is already but must seek what it is yet to be. It is better because the demands placed upon it are greater.

Just as meeting a responsibility increases the capacity for response, the improvement of a program reaffirms the importance of improvement. And so the process of becoming, which is the essence of education, continues. Many things are needed to build an honors program and to make it better. It should have admission standards and course requirements and a talented faculty and good support staff. It should have newsletters and reading lists for its students, as well as workshops and seminars for its faculty. Honors students should have their own living space and their own study space, including a computer lab and an honors library adorned with portraits of the world's great thinkers. An honors program should be able to sponsor a speakers series and other education events, such as conferences, films, and concerts. However, in the light of the foregoing, it becomes clear that there is far more to an honors program than office space, a letterhead, and a brochure of elevated policies and procedures.

Indeed, there is nothing of what meets the eye that may signify the element of *honors* in an honors program. The notion of an honors program remains just that — and idea, a concern for the truth, an embrace of the sacred, all of which are continually sought but never consummated. Thus it turns out that the issue concerning the image and essence of honors must remain unsettled, relegated to the realm of the yet-to-be that guides the quest undertaken. In its image and essence the honors program is not what it is but what it is in the process of becoming, what it is *not yet*. What Jacques Lacan says of the living individual, then, also is true of the life of the honors program: "What is realized in my history is not the past definite of what was. . . but the future anterior of what I shall have been for what I am in the process of becoming" (1968, p. 63). To cease becoming, to recall Bakhtin's remark, means spiritual death. If the honors program represents anything in the community of higher education, it is spiritual life. If, as the site of the highest in educational aspiration, the honors program does not stand for spiritual life, no other program will. And higher education will be void of all higher concern.

* * *

Like any discourse intended for the well being of its subject matter, these comments apply more to what ought to be than to what is. No doubt there are students enrolled and professors teaching in honors programs who do not live up to the ideals presented here. But if we are to go anywhere with what is — if the image is to take on meaning and the essence to assume substance — then we must address the *not yet* of what *ought* to be. Everything discussed here — the relation between life and learning, the testimony of teaching, the consecration that characterizes true education — makes the question of the image and essence of honors a matter of utmost urgency, one that decides our own image and essence.

What we are lies very much in what education means to us, and what education means to us rests largely on what honors means to us. If honors is to stand for the honor that it signifies, then it must assume the integrity that honor entails. The wholeness implied by integrity is a wholeness that comes when word and meaning, image and essence, are of a piece. They are joined in the ultimate concern and the moment of insight that occurs *between* two souls, between a student and a professor dialogically engaged in a quest for the truth.

141

Therefore, an honors program is not something we have but something we make happen, from one encounter to the next. It is not a structure within a network of services but an event that is forever in the process of unfolding.

On the Essence of Teaching

Said the Sufi Gurgani, "The teacher and the taught together produce the teaching" (Shah 1968, p. 164). This deceptively simple insight suggests a view of teaching and its essence that is rather unlike the views of teaching that one often finds, for example, in colleges of education. There teaching is frequently regarded as a certain skill required to pass on information, and student teachers are assessed on the basis of their effectiveness, their methods, their use of audiovisual aids, and so on.

However, the Sufi Gurgani suggests that teaching, both as a verb and as a noun, is something else, something akin to the birth of a presence resulting from the coming together of two parties. "Midwifery," as Allan Bloom argues, "describes teaching more adequately than does the word socialization" (1987, p. 20). The event of teaching does more than make some adjustments to an existing life; it adds to life a depth that had not been there before, imparting new substance and meaning, new hopes and horizons, to the living human being. Yet midwifery is perhaps not an altogether adequate analogy, for in the process of teaching both the student and the teacher are born anew. And something more is born between them.

Therefore, teaching is not just something a person does, as if it were an action that belonged to him alone. Viewed simply as an activity that one engages in, teaching often becomes a matter of method, a question of psychology, or a concern for strategy — everything except the engendering of a relation between one human soul and another. Lesson plans and methodologies, stated objectives and projected outcomes, filmstrips and field trips — all of these are useful and have their place. But when teaching is reduced to such props and projects, a danger arises of objectifying and thus obscuring the face of the one before whom we stand when we enter the classroom. Approached in terms of a face-to-face encounter, teaching assumes the aspects of dialogical relation, rather than monological instruction. The authority of the instructor is abrogated and ascribed to the authority of truth.

Viewing teaching in terms of dialogical encounter also raises certain phenomenological and existential issues regarding the nature of that encounter. Abraham Joshua Heschel, for example, insists:

> Everything depends on the person who stands in front of the classroom. The teacher is not an automatic fountain from which intellectual beverages may be obtained. He is either a witness or a stranger. To guide a pupil into the promised land, he must have been there himself. When asking himself: Do I stand for what I teach? Do I believe what I say? he must be able to answer in the affirmative. (1983, pp. 62-63)

Perhaps we should soften Heschel's statement by saying that, if the teacher has not been to the promised land, he or she at least must be seeking it. In any case, what the teacher offers to the student is not just information or knowledge but his or her very life as a testimony to what there is to hold dear in life.

Teaching is a form of living, a form of dwelling that creates a place in which the other human being may dwell. That is how community happens. Teaching is the antidote to spiritual exile and existential homelessness. It is a constitutive feature of the movement of return. Thinkers as varied as the Sufi Gurgani and Rabbi Heschel thus suggest that teaching is not an activity performed by an individual, but an event that both includes and transcends individual action. It is the opening of a door to life that transpires in a space *between* a teacher and a student. It is a process of listening and response, an offering up of the self to the other and for the other, by which both are transformed.

And, to the extent that truth is of interest to those involved in the event, teaching occurs between two in the light of a mutual, implied relation to a Third. Therefore, says Franz Rosenzweig, "Teaching begins where the subject matter ceases to be subject matter and changes into inner power" (1955, p. 76). Inner power leads to higher truth. In teaching, as in life, *within* and *above* are synonyms. What Karl Jaspers says of thinking, then, also applies to teaching: "In thinking, something which is not this thought itself awakens" (1959, p. 47). In teaching, something that is not reducible to this subject matter is revealed. In teaching, student and teacher come together to open up a path to a Third that belongs to neither and yet consecrates both. Therefore, let us consider these three reference points that delineate the ramifications of teaching viewed as encounter: the student, the teacher, and the Third.

The Student

Who is this young man or woman, this little boy or girl, this student laden with an armload of books? It is the being who, through the event of teaching, is made manifest as *child*. As the one whose name we utter with tones of love — as the soul entrusted to our care — the child is the one whom we teach and therefore whom we embrace. Like the little boy lost in William Blake's *Songs of Innocence*, the child cries out to us:

> Father, father, where are you going?
> O do not walk so fast.
> Speak father, speak to your little boy,
> Or else I shall be lost.

The pursuit of the father and the fear of being lost underlie the eagerness and devotion of the student. Indeed these are connotations of the Latin present participle *studere*, from which the word *student* is derived. "Speak to your little boy" is as much as to say, "Teach your little boy." As we respond to this summons, to this child's eagerness and devotion, we become teachers, and our children become students.

Moreover, underlying the teaching endeavor is the premise that the child as student — and the student as child — embodies everything we hold dear through a revelation of time, and therefore of potentiality; through an announcement of what is yet to be for the other *human* being. Emmanuel Levinas describes this time that is the student's time when he says:

> To be for a time that would be without me, for a time after my time, over and beyond the celebrated "being for death," is not an ordinary thought which is extrapolating from my own duration; it is the passage to the time of the other. (1987*a*, p. 92)

Meaning lies in this yet-to-be that belongs to the other person, to the student. Meaning implies direction, and to have a direction is to have a place, a horizon, where we have yet to arrive. It is in this sense that "time is essentially a new birth," as Levinas expresses it (1987*b*, p. 81). It is the birth of the student that opens up for the teacher the prospect of a new birth by pointing the teacher toward the horizon to which he or she would guide the student. Thus oriented toward a realm where he or she has yet to arrive, the student is movement itself. The student signifies the process — the present participle — of becoming that sustains life itself.

Thus understood, the student is the one who is opposed to death. It is written in the Agada of the Babylonian Talmud that as long as King David was engaged in study, in this process of becoming, the Angel of Death had no power over him (*En Jacob* 1918-22, vol. 1, p. 119). At stake in the student's endeavor is his spiritual life or death, and this is what gives us a stake in our own lives.

Approached from this urgency surrounding what is *not yet,* the student is the living nexus where the canons and traditions of the past take on substance through a link with the future. Indeed, when left to lie between the covers of a book, the text of the already said that characterizes the past is merely the dead flesh of meaning. It takes on life only as we engage it. For as we engage it, the text engages us and takes on a future that distinguishes human life. The future of human life, again, is rooted in the child.

As a figure of the child, the student signifies and thus imparts significance to the future; he or she is the trace of that open horizon of possibility and promise. Why do we keep track of our alumni? It is not just for their dollars. More than that, it is because we long for a glimpse of the time that is not our time, of the future as it had been for those who were once our students. It is because we want to see whether some small part of the world has been redeemed or made better as a result of our teaching. The basis of teaching is not simply the financial or social well-being of the student. It is not to enable the student to "get more out of life," as many suppose, but to enable him or her to impart more to life. Or perhaps it would be better to say that, because teaching is for the well-being of the student, it is for the well-being of all who are yet to surround the student.

Therefore, one can see that there is a certain messianic element at work in teaching. One can understand why Levinas declares, "The teacher-pupil relationship does not consist in communicating ideas to one another. It is the first radiant sign of messianism itself" (1990*a*, p. 86). And one can understand why Elie Wiesel writes, "The Messiah. We seek him, we pursue him. We think he is in heaven; we don't know that he likes to come down as a child. And yet, every man's childhood is messianic in essence" (1973*b*, p. 132). These words, indeed, are steeped in a tradition that attaches a certain messianic significance to the child as student. "The world would not be sustained," it is written in the *En Jacob,* "if it were not for the breath of [praise coming forth from] the school children" (vol. 1, p. 196). One begins to sense the gravity and the immensity of what is placed in a teacher's hands, because it is a charge as boundless as the future.

The future orientation that the student brings to teaching casts him or her in the role not only of learner but, more important, of seeker. As such, the student is in a constant state of motion, forever engaged in a quest for what is never at hand in the past or present. Thus undertaking the quest, the student is defined more by the *questions* that sustain this movement than by the answers that interrupt it. The wisdom sought fuels the search, as Levinas reminds us: "What enables the soul to rise to truth is nourished with truth" (1969, p. 114). This is a variation on the teaching that in the midst of the Hebrew word for "question," *she'elah*, is the *el* that is one of the names of God. The One we seek abides in the questions we ask — often in the form of another question.

Moreover, the 13th-century mystic, Rabbi Joseph Gikatilla, notes that "often in the Torah the attribute EL is called *CheSeD* [loving kindness]" and that "God created the world with *CheSeD*" (1994, p. 276). This implies that the student who is engaged in the process of quest and questioning is participating in the creation. Creation is a process of introducing order and orientation where there is disorientation. Cast in the mode of questioning, the student's orientation toward the future is a disorientation: To be a student is to feel oneself lost, which is the first step toward feeling the essence of one's self or soul.

José Ortega y Gasset addresses this aspect of the student's condition, which is a manifestation of a basic human condition, when he says, "It is not that man happens to be disoriented, to be losing himself in life, but that, insofar as one can see, man's situation, his life, in itself is disorientation, is being lost" (1969, p. 27). This condition of being lost that is so critical to the student's endeavor can be more than disorienting — it can be horrifying. The darkness of the void penetrates the cracks of fixed phrases and ready answers. Yet, as Ortega y Gasset suggests, it is only when we feel our self or soul slipping away that we take on the depth required for the calling of deep unto deep.

That call is just what is encountered in the teaching event, and it resonates from the face of the child who stands face to face with the teacher. To teach is to come before the countenance, and this encounter with the face is what makes teaching a dialogical endeavor. "Face and discourse are tied," Levinas states. "The face speaks. It speaks, it is in this that it renders possible and begins all discourse" (1985, pp. 87-88). To put it differently, face and word are tied. What begins again and ever again in the teaching encounter is precisely the word. Inasmuch as questioning sustains the movement of the quest, it sustains the utterance of the word in the dialogical interaction of hearing and response that determines the presence of those involved in the encounter. Leonard Grob argues:

> The genuine teacher, then, invites dialogue in the course of acknowledging his or her "presumption to know." In this sense, teachers model "teachability" for their students. What the Socratic teacher comes to teach, ultimately, is no fixed body of knowledge or skill; what she or he comes to teach is the desire to be taught! At bottom, what distinguishes the teacher from the student is that the former knows better than the latter the need to lead an examined life. (1993, p. 7)

Bloom comments on this condition that Grob describes, noting that:

> such experience is a condition of investigating *the* question, "What is man?," in relation to his highest aspirations as opposed to his low and common needs. A liberal education precisely means helping students to pose this question to themselves, to become aware that the answer is neither obvious nor simply unavailable, and that there is no serious life in which this question is not a continuous concern. (1987, p. 21)

Because it is a continuous concern, the question is as real for the teacher as it is for the student. Deep calls unto deep, from both sides of the dialogue, from generation to generation. "Somewhere," said Rabbi Nachman of Breslov, "there lives a man who asks a question to which there is no answer; a generation later, in another place, there lives a man who asks another question to which there is no answer either — and he doesn't know, he cannot know, that *his* question is actually an answer to the first" (Wiesel 1978, p. 158). Such "answers" are ever-changing, but the primal question underlying them all remains essentially the same.

What, then, is the call of deep unto deep? It is the first question put to the first man — Where are you? — for the examined life inheres in the ability to hear this question. Because teaching is not couched in the student or in the teacher but takes place dialogically between the two, the question confronts both. The one who stands before a student must stand for something and must therefore summon from himself or herself the response that he or she would summon from the student. The teacher is the student *par excellence*. Thus, as the child begets the man, so does the student teach the one who would teach him. "I learned much from my teachers," a Talmudic sage once said, "more, however, from my colleagues, but from my disciples, I learned the most" (*En Jacob* 1918-22, vol. 5, pp. 112-13). The "I" goes out to the other in order to return with a self. "Until I see the other," Wiesel has expressed it, "I cannot be I" (Wiesel and O'Connor 1990, p. 48). And so the student as other fashions the I of the teacher in the teaching encounter. Who, we now ask, is this I?

The Teacher

If teaching is not an activity but an event that occurs within a dialogical encounter, then the teacher is not one who merely dictates or trains but, above all, is one who responds. As a teacher, he or she responds prior to the student having uttered anything, declaring by his or her very presence, "Before you call, I shall answer." The teacher is the one who initiates the dialogical interaction by responding to the summons to teach, to the soul within and beyond that cries, "Speak, or I shall be lost!"

In the words of Allan Bloom, "There is no real teacher who in practice does not believe in the existence of the soul, or in a magic that acts on it through speech" (1987, p. 20). And so Elie Wiesel raises a rhetorical question: "Isn't this the dream of . . . any teacher — to find words that will sing and dance, words that will burn?" (1991, p. 251). Words that burn arise from a soul on fire; they teem with meaning and intensity. Teaching is an instance of the "enkindling," to use Karl Jaspers' term, that happens "in the contact of the soul with Being" and through which "Being

150

acquires communicative power" (1959, pp. 39-40). When the teacher speaks with words that burn, life itself speaks.

If teaching is viewed in terms of dialogue — if it transpires through words that burn — then one must teach not just from texts, charts, or overhead projections but from the heart and soul of oneself. This presence of the human soul in the teaching situation is what makes it a *living* situation, constituted not only by individual lives but by life as such. This is what lends the situation itself a *face*. This is how spirit unfolds — not the "Spirit of the Times," not the *Zeitgeist,* but the spirit that is mind, that is *Geist* itself. That is what manifests itself where teaching happens.

"The soul," Mikhail Bakhtin explains, "is an image of the totality of all that is truly experienced, of all that is at hand, in the soul in time; spirit, however, is the totality of all meaning, of all significant direction in life" (1979, p. 97). However, the totality that is spirit is an open-ended totality; it is the totality of the infinite. The dialogical interaction that distinguishes teaching implies a relation to the infinite, which is a relation to the spirit residing in a third position between two. "Every encounter suggests infinity," writes Elie Wiesel. "Which means: the self is linked to infinity only through the intermediary of another self, another consciousness" (1973*b*, p. 88). But we shall examine this point in more detail later. For now let it be noted that the primary function of the teacher is not to provide ready answers, nor is it simply to ask questions. The teacher's main task is to impart responsibility — that is, response-ability, response capacity. To do this, he or she must develop an ever-deepening capacity for response. It is in that ever-deepening capacity that a trace of the infinite shows itself.

Such a capacity requires not only one who is adept at speech and explanation but also one who is able to listen in an actively responsive manner to the call of life that comes both from the student and from beyond the student. In short, the teacher must become a living soul by answering a summons, as one might answer a subpoena. What is the one thing that can guarantee the "inner bonding" of the elements of one's personality, by which the soul comes to life? "Only," says Bakhtin, "the wholeness of responsibility" (1979, p. 5). The substance and significance of the teacher as a living soul is established through his or her responsibility to and for the student, through the responsibility that reveals itself in the dialogical relation to the student. Hence one does not imply two; rather, two are necessary to constitute the wholeness of one. Therefore, Levinas asserts, "Subjectivity is the other in the same. . . . The other in the same determinative of subjectivity is the restlessness of the same disturbed by the other" (1981, p. 25).

Subjectivity lies not in solipsistic isolation but in dialogical relation. Subjectivity is responsibility; consciousness is restlessness. But restlessness can produce anxiety, and anxiety can render the teacher prone to temptation. In the context of teaching, the temptation is to allow the text or the prescribed method (the script contrived and ready-made) to speak for us and thus to eclipse our human presence. The painful labor is deciding who we are and what we stand for. If the teacher must be a good listener, the organ by which he or she hears is the tongue; whether speaking or listening, we hear by responding. "He who ceases to make a response," Martin Buber states it, "ceases to hear the Word" (1965, p. 45).

Furthermore, just as the teacher questions the student, so does the student — both implicitly and explicitly — question the teacher, not only about a given subject but about his or her very essence. If we begin learning only when we begin teaching, it is not merely because we must master a subject in order to explain it. Additionally, it is because through teaching we begin to learn something about ourselves, about why we live and die, about what we hold dear. This happens because we must become responsible. For responsibility means that we cannot decide something about a given subject without also deciding something about ourselves.

With this deciding comes the awakening characterized by the student's disturbance of the teacher. Moreover, this awakening entails not only the opening of the eyes but also an opening of a wound. Responding to the student, the human being becomes a teacher; becoming a teacher, he or she is wounded. To borrow once more from Levinas, the extreme difficulty and discomfort surrounding the teacher's responsibility lie in the fact that "the other calls upon that sensitivity with a vocation that wounds, calls upon an irrevocable responsibility, and thus the very identity of a subject. Signification is witness or martyrdom" (1981, pp. 77-78).

And so is teaching. One cannot teach without caring, and one cannot care without hurting. The question is: What does this caring and hurting attest to? To come before the face is to be called to the stand and to take a stand. The one who stands before a class cannot escape standing for something and is compelled to bear witness to something. Teaching is testimony. As the one who stands for something — as the one in responsibility — the teacher not only is a giver of signs but is a sign. He or she may choose to flee to the formula or to answer with his or her life, but the teacher cannot choose whether or not to be called. This condition of being chosen before choosing is what makes teaching a vocation, a calling that draws the teacher forth in such a way that he or she is no longer free *not* to teach.

From beyond the face of the student there comes a commandment. "It orders me," in the words of Levinas, "as one orders someone one commands, as when one says: 'Someone's asking for you'" (1985, p. 98). This asking, this calling upon the teacher, can wound because, as one who is in a position of responsibility, the teacher is responsible for the error and the suffering of the student. To become a self is to become a subject, and to become a subject is to be subjected, taking upon oneself the wounds of the other. Thus the teacher is not the one who whines, "I suffer, therefore I am," but the one who in gladness affirms, "I suffer, therefore you are." In this way the difference between self and other, between teacher and student, is transformed into non-indifference.

Thus the witness born by the teacher becomes an affirmation of what there is to care about, of what there is to love. The urgency underlying the teaching encounter lies in the fact that what is most precious in life also is most fragile. "Like a new-born child," to recall Buber's metaphor for the educational encounter (1965, p. 114), it must be carefully nurtured, protected, and, above all, affirmed. If teaching is testimony, it also is affirmation, a yea-saying when saying yes to life is most difficult, as it must seem to be in this destitute time, when suicide is one of the leading causes of death among teenagers.

Teaching is itself a form of praise and a form of healing. The teacher affirms life's wellspring of joy and wonder. "We teach children how to measure," Heschel laments, "how to weigh. We fail to teach them how to revere, how to sense wonder and awe" (1955, p. 36). It is neither power nor greed that is at the "root of our sin," the Rabbi argues, but "indifference to the sublime wonder of living" (p. 43). It is indifference to the wonder of living that results in the horror of living death. A life-and-death endeavor, teaching is a process of re-establishing life's attachment to life by transforming indifference into concern, despair into joy, negation into affirmation; and this introduces to the educational encounter a certain religious aspect. It makes education into an instance of *chinuch,* to use the Hebrew term, which, we recall, means both "education" and "consecration." Called forth, the teacher is called on to generate an attachment of life to life and thereby to consecrate life through his or her dialogical encounter with the student.

Or better, it is not exactly that the teacher must connect life with life, but that he must become the connection in the midst of his relation and his testimony to the student, before the Most High. "For Judaism," Levinas states it in religious terms, "the goal of education consists in instituting a link between man and the saintliness of God and in maintaining man in this relationship" (1990*a*, p. 14). While the student is the place where the knot is tied between past and future, between question and response, the teacher is the one who does the tying through his or her affirmation of the dearness of the bond.

Once again, with the notion of a bond we have the idea of the *between,* of the realm where the teaching encounter occurs. This is the shifting site where teacher and student establish their presence in the teaching situation, where each struggles to answer the question, "Where are you?" with a cry of "Here I am," no sooner answering than having to answer again. Thus the self that the teacher must become is neither here nor there but in a *between* space that is constantly moving *elsewhere*. And the truth of the encounter — the truth that lends substance and meaning to the encounter — is the truth of the self.

The effort to declare one's presence with a voicing of "Here I am" is an effort to become the truth: Teaching must be lived, every hour of every day. It transpires not only in the classroom but in one's office, up and down the halls, out on the street, and in the living room. But because teaching is an encounter that takes place between teacher and student, the truth that constitutes each lies outside of both. Like spirit, it is elsewhere.

"Teaching," Levinas maintains, "is a way for truth to be produced such that it is not my work, such that I could not derive it from my own interiority" (1969, p. 295). If the truth is regarded as nothing more than a matter of opinion or as an issue of power surrounding a subjective agenda — if one insists that "there are truths but no truth" — then there can be no teaching. What remains is, at best, only a contrived project of indoctrination. To cite Bakhtin, "Truth is not born nor is it to be found inside the head of an individual person, it is born *between people* collectively searching for truth" (1984, p. 110). This brings us to the third element in the teaching encounter.

The Third

"When I write," Elie Wiesel has said, "I feel my invisible teachers looking over my shoulders, reading my words and judging their veracity" (Wiesel and de Saint-Cheron 1990, p. 173). The teacher addressing the student is not the first to teach; the teacher has had teachers of his or her own. In the dialogical conjunction of student and teacher there is always another teacher. Hence "in the Talmud," Levinas notes, for example, "it is always of great importance to specify, for each saying, who said it. A true teaching is one in which the universal nature of the truth it announces does not obliterate the name or the identity of the person who said it" (1989*b*, p. 225).

Approaching this idea from a slightly different perspective, in his examination of dialogical discourse Bakhtin argues that "every dialogue proceeds as though against the background of a third who is invisibly present, standing above all the participants in the dialogue. . . . It is a constitutive feature of the whole expression" (1979, p. 306). And it will be recalled that in his psychoanalytic scheme Jacques Lacan employs the concept of the Other in his investigation of the interchange between one person and another, explaining that "the Other with a big 'O' is the scene of the Word insofar as the scene of the Word is always in third position between two subjects. This is only to introduce the dimension of Truth" (1968, p. 269). This third position — what we here refer to as "the Third"— is the ground of meaning for the student who is a vessel of the yet-to-be and for the teacher who attests to the dearness of life. It is the Third that elevates teaching from an activity requiring skill to an encounter demanding testimony. As Wiesel, Levinas, Bakhtin, and Lacan suggest, each in his own way, the Third imparts to the encounter all the urgency of a truth that is yet to be decided, yet to be revealed.

If, as Bakhtin has said, "for me, memory is memory of the future" (1979, p. 110), such memory is a mindfulness of the truth that lies above and beyond me, calling me forth to begin and bear witness again and ever again. The truth is situated in a third position because neither the teacher nor the student stands in the privileged position of the truth. Only from this position of the Third can the truth of the teacher in his or her relation to the student come into question. Thus the *who* of the teacher is inextricably bound to his or her relation to the Third. One of Lacan's insights from his essay, "The Agency of the Letter," comes to mind in this connection:

> Who, then, is this other to whom I am more attached than
> to myself, since, at the heart of my assent to my own identi-

ty it is still he who agitates me? . . . This other is the Other.
(1977, p. 172)

If, as Bloom holds, *the* question decided in the event of teaching is "What is man?" (1987, p. 21), it is a question that can be decided only through an awareness of our relation to this third presence. Yet it is never decided once and for all; that is what makes teaching and learning an eternally ongoing endeavor. "The ultimate word of the world and about the world has not yet been spoken," Bakhtin insists. "Everything is still in the future and will always be in the future" (1984, p. 166). This places the truth of everything in a third position, silent and invisible, not only spatially but temporally, or better, infinitely and eternally. The Third is invisibly present because He is present as an eternal question, whose secret is couched in the silence of the future. The Third is invisibly present because, in the question that distinguishes the dialogue between student and teacher, He is silently present — and as omnipresent as silence itself.

This notion of a third presence between or above the student and teacher engaged in a dialogical pursuit of the truth is not as alien as it may seem at first glance. What — or who — is this Third? Lacan, as we have noted, calls it the Other; Bakhtin describes the Third as "the overman, the over-*I* — that is, the witness and judge of every person (of every *I*)" (1979, p. 342). In *I and Thou,* Buber alludes to this third presence when he says, "Through every single You the basic word [I-Thou] addresses the eternal You" (p. 123). Nor is this concept confined to modern thought.

Indeed, it is as old as the search for the truth. Rabbi Chananiah ben Teradion, for example, is cited in the Talmud as having declared that when two come together in study of the Torah, with the holy Word passing "between them," the "[Divine] Presence is with them" (*Avot* 3:2). In the 7th-century *Midrash Tanchuma* we read, "Said Rabbi Yitschak: When those of flesh and blood build a palace, they first build the lower part, and then they build the upper part. But the Holy One, blessed be He, first created the

157

upper part [the heavens] and then created the lower part [the earth]" (1935, vol. 1, p. 9). Why? Because only the upper part — the dimension of the higher, of the sacred, of the truth — can lend significance to the lower part. And what fashions both parts, we are taught, is the Torah (*Midrash Tanchuma*, vol. 1, p. 1).

That is why the *Shekhinah,* or the Presence of the Third, enters wherever a student and a teacher are gathered in its name. The word *Torah,* it will be recalled, means "teaching," and it is commonly referred to with the metaphors of *light* and *life.* The Torah, in fact, is known as the *Ets Chaim,* or the "Tree of Life." When it occurs in the light of the Third, teaching becomes not only an affirmation of life but of its origin and therefore of all that the Torah signifies. Where teaching transpires, life *happens.* Levinas states it even more powerfully, asserting that "the apparition of a third party is the very origin of appearing, that is, the very origin of an origin" (1981, p. 160). The Third, then, is both the ground and the goal of teaching, its point of departure and point of return.

Teaching is precisely a movement of return, a *teshuvah*, to borrow the Hebrew term. I introduce the Hebrew word to our discussion of the Third because it sheds helpful light on what is at work here. For *teshuvah* means not only "return" but also "redemption" and "response." In its affirmation of life, teaching redeems life from the terrible forces of negation and despair, from the meaninglessness and nothingness that threaten life whenever the relation to the Third is lost. Therefore "*teshuvah* is more than just repentance from sin," Adin Steinsaltz points out. "It is a spiritual reawakening, a desire to strengthen the connection between oneself and the sacred" (1987, p. 3).

The sacred, in the terms we are using here, is the Third. When linked with the concept of the Third, the notion of *teshuvah* also helps us to see that the response and responsibility of teaching as a dialogical relation include a higher relation as well. Answering to my student, I answer to Another, who is the Sacred, with my life for the dearness of all life; it is my accountability to the Third that gives meaning to my relation to my student. And, apart from this higher responsibility, there can be no higher education. For the Third lays claim to me from above.

In our age one of the most common alibis that has desecrated teaching and eclipsed the face of the Third — and with it the face of the student — is careerism, money, the marketplace. The merchants have invaded the Temple and have made teaching into its very opposite, into a business. More than ever, the true task of the teacher is to make manifest the higher being and the higher responsibility that instill education with what is higher, making it into a movement of return, which is a movement of ascent, an *aliyah.* What is this ascent toward? The answer is the Good, which, Levinas holds, "is not the object of a choice, for it has taken possession of the subject before the subject had the time — that is, the distance — necessary for choice. There is indeed no subjection more complete than this possession by the Good, this election" (1987*a*, pp. 134-35). To teach is to join our voice to the Voice of the Good that lays claim to us in a saying of *ki tov,* of "it is very good." It is good to ask, good to seek, good to teach and to learn, because there is a Third from whom life derives its meaning.

Hence there is no dwelling, no living, without this event of teaching. But how, it will be asked, is the Third made manifest in teaching? How does it reveal itself? Here, too, the thinkers we have drawn on may be of some help. In words that apply perfectly to the event we are examining, Levinas, for instance, writes:

> The witness testifies to what was said by himself. For he has said "Here I am!" before the Other; and from the fact that before the Other he recognizes the responsibility which is incumbent upon himself, he has manifested what the face of the Other signified for him. The glory of the Infinite reveals itself through what it is capable of doing in the witness. (1985, p. 109)

The quest for the truth that is yet to be is the "proof" of its presence in the movement of the quest; that there is a flame that ignites the soul is "demonstrated" by the soul on fire, aflame with the affirmation of life that makes teaching *matter.* Lacan addresses this issue of how teaching establishes the presence of the Third by saying, "I can only just prove to the Other that he exists, not, of course, with the proofs for the existence of God with which over the centuries he has been killed off, but by loving him" (1977, p. 317). Just to allay any possible confusion on this point, it must be noted, as Buber notes, that love is not a feeling. Buber argues:

> Feelings one 'has'; love occurs. Feelings dwell in man, but man dwells in his love. This is no metaphor but actuality: love does not cling to an I, as if the You were merely its 'content' or object; it is between I and You. . . . Love is responsibility of an I for a You: in this consists what cannot consist in any feeling. (1970, p. 66)

Likewise, as we have seen, teaching occurs and announces itself as responsibility; it is between teacher and student and a Third. For the love that happens in the midst of teaching manifests itself as a third, living presence. Once again I come up against the fact that I cannot teach without caring for those whom I teach, whether I like it or not. It is through my love for the student, as an expression of my love for the Good, that I signify what it means to be a teacher. And this love is commanded: Someone is asking for you. Love is asking for you.

Thus in our reflection on teaching we are finally led to the religious language of "love for that which is all love," as Henri Bergson describes religious life (1954, p. 212). The quest for truth, the summons to testimony, the responsibility to and for the Third — all of it is steeped in a love for life and for that which transcends life. And so Levinas asks, "Is love a pleasant, tactile sensation, or a way to still seek him who is nonetheless as close as he can be? But is it an absence? Is it not the presence of infinity?" (1987a, p. 122). The process of teaching is just such a seeking, and it derives its substance from just such a presence. What is teaching? It is a sublime form of loving, sublime because it unveils the presence of the infinite.

A Closing Remark

On 20 January 1942 Reinhard Heydrich, head of the Nazi SS Intelligence, convened the Wannsee Conference in a suburb of Berlin. The purpose of the Conference was to work out the details of the Final Solution to the Jewish Problem. Of the 14 men who attended that meeting, eight held doctorate degrees, and nearly all were educated in the finest universities of Central Europe. Hence it came to pass that men of culture and learning gathered to plot the murder of a people, including the children. Indeed, the children were specifically marked for annihilation in a calculated, step-by-step fashion, beginning with their expulsion from their schools. Removing them from their teachers was the first step toward exterminating them from the world, which, according to Jewish tradition, subsists thanks to the children. And, according to the view here set forth, children subsist thanks to teaching.

But, as the Wannsee Conference demonstrates, when teaching is drained of a relation to the Third, when it is reduced to technological training, when it is no more than a preparation for successful careers or political maneuvering — children die. This is no exaggeration. Nor is it an issue confined to Wannsee. Those who currently are involved in education are all too familiar with the push to foster science, math, and other technological pursuits, or to recast the curriculum in the politically correct mold of gender studies, ethnic studies, and studies of "alternative lifestyles." There is nothing wrong with the study of these areas as such; but when they are pursued in the absence of other studies — in the absence of any higher or deeper embrace of human life and human sanctity — then they lead to death. Such training or indoctrination, to be sure, is not education at all. It has nothing to do with the consecration that the Hebrew word *chinuch* suggests, no connection to what there is to sanctify and thus to love. And this is what teaching is about.

The event of loving embrace that distinguishes teaching is a consecration of life through a testimony and pursuit of the sacred, for the sake of all that is sacred. However, simply asserting this is not enough. It is needful but not sufficient. From here we must return once more to begin again and ever again. Though the task has been met a million times, it remains forever yet to be done; for the debt increases in the measure that it is paid. And so, having said this, let us return to our students for the encounter that lends life meaning.

BIBLIOGRAPHY

Abrabanel, Don Isaac. *Abrabanel on Pirke Avot.* Compiled and translated by Abraham Chill. New York: Sepher-Hermon, 1991.

Appelfeld, Aharon. *First-Person Essays.* Jerusalem: Zionist Library, 1979.

Arad, Yitzhak; Gutman, Yisrael; and Margaloit, Abraham, eds. "Protocol of the Wannsee Conference, January 20, 1942." In *Documents on the Holocaust,* edited by Yitzhak Arad, Yisrael Gutman, and Abraham Margaloit. Jerusalem: Yad Vashem, 1981.

Aristotle. *Politica.* Translated by Benjamin Jowett. In *Introduction to Aristotle,* edited Richard McKeon. New York: Modern Library, 1947.

Auden, W.H. "In Memory of W.B. Yeats." In *The Major Poets: English and American,* 2nd ed., edited by Charles M. Coffin and Gerrit Hubbard Roelofs. New York: Harcourt Brace Jovanovich, 1969.

Auden, W.H. "September 1, 1939." In *The Major Poets: English and American,* 2nd ed., edited by Charles M. Coffin and Gerrit Hubbard Roelofs. New York: Harcourt Brace Jovanovich, 1969.

Augustine. *On Free Choice of the Will.* Translated by Thomas Williams. Indianapolis: Hackett, 1993.

Bakhtin, Mikhail. *Estetika slovesnogo tvorchestva.* Moscow: Isskustvo, 1979.

Bakhtin, Mikhail. *The Dialogic Imagination.* Edited by Michael Holquist. Translated by Caryl Emerson and Michael Holquist. Austin: University of Texas Press, 1981.

Bakhtin, Mikhail. *Problems of Dostoevsky's Poetics.* Translated by Caryl Emerson. Minneapolis: University of Minnesota Press, 1984.

Bakhtin, Mikhail. *Art and Answerability,* edited by Michael Holquist and Vadim Liapunov. Translated by Vadim Liapunov. Austin: University of Texas Press, 1990.

Bennett, William J. "America's Revolt Against God." *Policy Review* 67 (Winter 1994): 19-26.

Berdyaev, Nicolas. *The Destiny of Man.* Translated by Natalie Duddington. New York: Harper & Row, 1960.

Bergson, Henri. *Two Sources of Morality and Religion.* Translated by R. Ashley Audra and Cloudsley Brereton. Garden City, N.Y.: Doubleday, 1954.

Blake, William. *Poems and Prophecies.* New York: Dutton, 1975.

Blanchot, Maurice. *The Writing of the Disaster.* Translated by Ann Smock. Lincoln: University of Nebraska Press, 1986.

Bloom, Allan. *The Closing of the American Mind.* New York: Simon and Schuster, 1987.

Bohr, Niels. *Atomic Theory and the Description of Nature.* Cambridge: Cambridge University Press, 1934.

Brown, Norman O. *Love's Body.* New York: Vintage, 1966.

Buber, Martin. *Between Man and Man.* Translated by Ronald Gregor Smith. New York: Macmillan, 1965.

Buber, Martin. *I and Thou.* Translated by Walter Kaufmann. New York: Charles Scribner's Sons, 1970.

Camus, Albert. *The Myth of Sisyphus and Other Essays.* Translated by Justin O'Brien. New York: Vintage Books, 1955.

Camus, Albert. *The Stranger.* Translated by Matthew Ward. New York: Vintage Books, 1988.

Cervantes, Miguel de. *Don Quixote of La Mancha.* Translated by Walter Starkie. New York: New American Library, 1979.

Chofetz Chaim. *Let There Be Light.* Translated by Raphael Blumberg. Jerusalem: Feldheim, 1992.

Conrad, Joseph. *Heart of Darkness.* New York: Washington Square, 1974.

Culi, Yaakov. *The Torah Anthology: MeAm Lo'ez.* Vol. 1. Translated by Aryeh Kaplan. New York: Maznaim, 1977.

Dante. *The Inferno.* Translated by John Ciardi. New York: New American Library, 1954.

Davis, Howard E. "Elitism and Honors: A Catechism and Some Propositions." *Forum for Honors* 19 (Fall 1989): 18-23.

Derrida, Jacques. "Like the Sound of the Deep Sea within a Shell: Paul de Man's War." *Critical Inquiry* 14 (1988): 590-652.

Descartes, Rene. *Meditations on First Philosophy.* Translated by Donald A. Cress. Indianapolis: Hackett, 1979.

Dostoevsky, F.M. *Neizdannyi Dostoevskii — Zapisnye knizhki i tetradi 1860-1868 gg.* In *Literaturnoe nasledstvo.* Vol. 30. Edited by V.R. Shcherbina. Moscow. Isskustvo, 1971.

Dostoevsky, F.M. *The Possessed.* Translated by Andrew R. MacAndrew. New York: New American Library, 1962.

Dostoevsky, F.M. *Notes from Underground.* Translated by Mirra Ginsburg. New York: Bantam Books, 1974.

Dostoevsky, F.M. *The Brothers Karamazov.* Translated by Constance Garnett. New York: New American Library, 1980.

Dostoevsky, F.M. *Winter Notes on Summer Impressions.* Translated by David Patterson. Evanston, Ill.: Northwestern University Press, 1988.

Edwards, Bruce L. "The Suicide of Liberal Education: Deconstruction in Academia." Heritage Lecture 277. Washington, D.C.: Heritage Foundation, 1990.

Ellis, John M. *Against Deconstruction.* Princeton, N.J.: Princeton University Press, 1989.

Eliot, T.S. *The Waste Land and Other Poems.* New York: Harcourt Brace Jovanovich, 1962.

Emerson, Ralph Waldo. *Selected Writings.* Edited by William H. Gilman. New York: New American Library, 1965.

En Jacob: Agada of the Babylonian Talmud. Translated by S. H. Glick. 5 Vols. New York: Hebrew Publishing Co., 1918-1922.

Ethics of the Fathers. Translated by Philip Blackman. New York: Judaica Press, 1985.

Fackenheim, Emil L. *The Jewish Return into History.* New York: Schocken, 1978.

Fackenheim, Emil L. *To Mend the World.* New York: Schocken, 1989.

Feuerbach, Ludwig. *The Essence of Christianity.* Translated by George Eliot. New York: Harper & Row, 1957.

Finkelstein, Louis. *Akiba: Scholar, Saint and Martyr.* New York: Atheneum, 1981.

Florensky, Pavel. *Stolp i utverzhdenie istiny.* Westmead, England: Gregg, 1970.

Freire, Paulo. *Cultural Action for Freedom.* Cambridge, Mass.: Harvard Educational Review and Center for the Study of Development and Social Change, 1970.

Frost, Robert. *Robert Frost's Poems.* New York: Washington Square, 1965.

165

Fruman, Norman. "Deconstruction, de Man, and the Resistance to Evidence: David Lehman's *Signs of the Times.*" *Academic Questions* 5 (Summer 1992): 34-47.

Gersonides. *The Wars of the Lord.* 2 vols. Translated by Seymour Feldman. Philadelphia: Jewish Publication Society, 1984.

Gikatilla, Joseph. *Sha'are Orah: Gates of Light.* Translated by Avi Weinstein. San Francisco: HarperCollins, 1994.

Ginott, Haim. *Teacher and Child: A Handbook for Parents and Teachers.* New York: Macmillan, 1972.

Goethe, Johann Wolfgang von. *Faust: Part 1.* Translated by C.F. MacIntyre. New York: New Directions, 1949.

Grob, Leonard. "Higher Education in the Shadows of the Holocaust." Paper presented at the 23rd annual meeting of the Scholars' Conference, Tulsa, Oklahoma, March 1993.

Grunberger, Richard. *The 12-Year Reich: A Social History of Nazi Germany, 1933-1945.* New York: Holt, Rinehart and Winston, 1971.

Heisenberg, Werner. *Physics and Philosophy.* New York: Harper & Row, 1954.

Heschel, Abraham Joshua. *God in Search of Man.* New York: Farrar Straus Giroux, 1955.

Heschel, Abraham Joshua. *The Earth Is the Lord's.* New York: Farrar Straus Giroux, 1978.

Heschel, Abraham Joshua. *I Asked for Wonder: A Spiritual Anthology.* Edited by Samuel H. Dresner. New York: Crossroad, 1983.

Hilberg, Raul. *The Destruction of the European Jews.* Chicago: Quadrangle Books, 1961.

Hirsch, David. *The Deconstruction of Literature: Criticism After Auschwitz.* Providence, R.I.: Brown University Press, 1992.

Hitler, Adolf. *Mein Kampf.* Translated by Ralph Manheim. Boston: Houghton Mifflin, 1971.

Homer. *The Odyssey.* Translated by W.H.D. Rouse. New York: Penguin, 1937.

Husserl, Edmund. *Phenomenology and the Crisis of Philosophy.* Translated by Quentin Lauer. New York: Harper, 1865.

Jabès, Edmond. *From the Desert to the Book.* Translated by Pierre Joris. Barrytown, N.Y.: Station Hill, 1990.

Jaspers, Karl. *Man in the Modern Age.* Translated by Eden and Cedar Paul. Garden City, N.Y.: Doubleday, 1957.

166

Jaspers, Karl. *Truth and Symbol*. Translated by Jean T. Wilde, William Kluback, and William Kimmel. New Haven, Conn.: College and University Press, 1959.

Jefferson, Thomas. "The Declaration of Independence." In *The Portable Thomas Jefferson*. Edited by Merrill D. Peterson. New York: Penguin, 1977.

Kahana, Rab. *Pesikta de-Rab Kahana*. Translated by William G. Braude and Israel J. Kapstein. Philadelphia: Jewish Publication Society, 1975.

Kaplan, Chaim A. *The Warsaw Diary of Chaim A. Kaplan*. Translated and edited by Abraham I. Katsh. New York: Collier Books, 1973.

Ka-tzetnik 135633. *Sunrise over Hell*. Translated by Nina De-Nur. London: W.H. Allen, 1977.

Kazantzakis, Nikos. *The Saviors of God: Spiritual Exercises*. Translated by Kimon Friar. New York: Simon and Schuster, 1960.

Kierkegaard, Søren. *Concluding Unscientific Postscript*. Translated by David F. Swenson and Walter Lowrie. Princeton, N.J.: Princeton University Press, 1941.

Kierkegaard, Søren. *The Concept of Dread*. Translated by Walter Lowrie. Princeton, N.J.: Princeton University Press, 1944. a

Kierkegaard, Søren. *Training in Christianity*. Translated by Walter Lowrie. Princeton, N.J.: Princeton University Press, 1944. b

Kierkegaard, Søren. *Fear and Trembling and the Sickness unto Death*. Translated by Walter Lowrie. Princeton, N.J.: Princeton University Press, 1968.

King, Martin Luther. *Why We Can't Wait*. New York: Harper & Row, 1964.

Kirk, Russell. "The Fraud of Multiculturalism." Heritage Lecture 396. Washington, D.C.: Heritage Foundation, 1992.

Kook, Abraham Isaac. *Orot*. Translated by Bezalel Naor. Northvale, N.J.: Aronson, 1993.

Kren, George M., and Rappoport, Leon. *The Holocaust and the Crisis of Human Behavior*. New York: Holmes and Meier, 1980.

Lacan, Jacques. *The Language of the Self*. Translated with commentary by Anthony Wilden. Baltimore: Johns Hopkins University Press, 1968.

Lacan, Jacques. *Ecrits*. Translated by Alan Sheridan. New York: W.W. Norton, 1977.

Levi, Primo. *The Drowned and the Saved*. Translated by Raymond Rosenthal. New York: Vintage Books, 1989.

167

Levinas, Emmanuel. *Totality and Infinity.* Translated by Alphonso Lingis. Pittsburgh: Duquesne University Press, 1969.

Levinas, Emmanuel. *Existence and Existents.* Translated by Alphonso Lingis. The Hague: Martinus Nijhoff, 1978.

Levinas, Emmanuel. *Otherwise Than Being or Beyond Essence.* Translated by Alphonso Lingis. The Hague: Martinus Nijhoff, 1981.

Levinas, Emmanuel. *Ethics and Infinity.* Translated by Richard Cohen. Pittsburgh: Duquesne University Press, 1985.

Levinas, Emmanuel. *Collected Philosophical Papers.* Translated by Alphonso Lingis. Dordrecht: Martinus Nijhoff, 1987. a

Levinas, Emmanuel. *Time and The Other.* Translated by Richard A. Cohen. Pittsburgh: Duquesne University Press, 1987. b

Levinas, Emmanuel. "The Paradox of Morality." Translated by Richard Cohen. In *The Provocation of Levinas: Rethinking the Other*, edited by Robert Bernasconi and David Ward. London: Routledge, 1988.

Levinas, Emmanuel. "Ethics as First Philosophy." Translated by Sean Hand and Michael Temple. In *The Levinas Reader*, edited by Sean Hand. Oxford: Basil Blackwell, 1989. a

Levinas, Emmanuel. "The Pact." Translated by Sarah Richmond. In *The Levinas Reader*, edited by Sean Hand. Oxford: Basil Blackwell, 1989. b

Levinas, Emmanuel. *Difficult Freedom: Essays on Judaism.* Translated by Sean Hand. Baltimore: Johns Hopkins University Press, 1990. a

Levinas, Emmanuel. *Nine Talmudic Readings.* Translated by Annette Aronowicz. Bloomington: Indiana University Press, 1990. b

Lindsay, Thomas K. "(Post)Modern Romance: Liberals and Multiculturalism." Heritage Lecture 463. Washington, D.C.: Heritage Foundation, 1993.

Littell, Franklin H. *The Crucifixion of the Jews.* Macon, Ga.: Mercer University Press, 1986.

Mansfield, Harvey C. "Political Correctness and the Suicide of the Intellect." Heritage Lecture 337. Washington, D.C.: Heritage Foundation, 1991.

Maimonides. *The Guide for the Perplexed.* Translated by M. Friedlaender. New York: Dover, 1956.

McDonald, Michael P. "Defending Academic Freedom." Heritage Lecture 371. Washington, D.C.: Heritage Foundation, 1992.

Midrash on Psalms. Translated by William G. Brauche. 2 Vols. New Haven, Conn.: Yale University Press, 1959.

Midrash Rabbah. Translated by A Cohen et al. 10 Vols. London: Soncino, 1961.

Midrash Tanchuma. 2 Vols. Jerusalem: Eshkol, 1935.

Milton, John. *Paradise Lost and Paradise Regained.* Edited by Christopher Ricks. New York: New American Library, 1968.

Nachman of Breslov. *Advice.* Translated by Avraham Greenbaum. Compiled by R. Nathan. Brooklyn: Breslov Research Institute, 1983.

National Commission on Excellence in Education. *A Nation at Risk: The Imperative for Educational Reform.* Washington, D.C.: U.S. Government Printing Office, 1983.

Nietzsche, Friedrich. *Beyond Good and Evil.* Translated by Walter Kaufmann. New York: Vintage Books, 1966.

Oppenheimer, Robert. *Science and the Common Understanding.* New York: Simon and Schuster, 1966.

Ortega y Gasset, José. *Some Lessons in Metaphysics.* Translated by Mildred Adams. New York: W.W. Norton, 1969.

Orwell, George. "Politics and the English Language." In *Exploring Language*, 3rd ed., edited by Gary Goshgarian. Boston: Little, Brown, 1983.

Osborne, John B. "Honors, Elitism, and the Iron Law of Oligarchy." *Forum for Honors* 19 (Fall 1989): 24-29.

Percy, Walker. *The Message in the Bottle.* New York: Farrar Straus and Giroux, 1982.

Plato. *Euthyphro.* Translated by Lane Cooper. In *The Collected Dialogues of Plato*, edited by Edith Hamilton and Hunting Cairns. Princeton, N.J.: Princeton University Press, 1961.

Plato. *Laws.* Translated by A.E. Taylor. In *The Collected Dialogues of Plato*, edited by Edith Hamilton and Hunting Cairns. Princeton, N.J.: Princeton University Press, 1961.

Plato. *Republic.* Translated by Paul Shorey. In *The Collected Dialogues of Plato*, edited by Edith Hamilton and Hunting Cairns. Princeton, N.J.: Princeton University Press, 1961.

Rand, Ayn. *The Virtue of Selfishness: A New Concept of Egoism.* New York: New American Library, 1964.

Rosenberg, Alan, and Myers, Gerald E., eds. *Echoes from the Holocaust: Philosophical Reflections on a Dark Time.* Philadelphia: Temple University Press, 1988.

Rosenzweig, Franz. *On Jewish Learning.* Edited and translated by N.N. Glatzer. New York: Schocken, 1955.

Rosenzweig, Franz. *The Star of Redemption*. Translated by William W. Hallo. Boston: Beacon, 1972.

Saadia Gaon. *The Book of Beliefs and Opinions*. Translated by Samuel Rosenblatt. New Haven, Conn.: Yale University Press, 1976.

Sachs, Nelly. *O the Chimneys*. Translated by Michael Hamburger et al. New York: Farrar Straus and Giroux, 1967.

Sandmel, Samuel. *Philo's Place in Judaism*. New York: Ktav, 1971.

Schirk, Heinz, director. *The Wannsee Conference*. A film produced by Rearguard, 1984.

Schneerson, Menachem M. *Torah Studies*. 2nd ed. Translated by Jonathan Sacks. London: Lubavitch Foundation, 1986.

Schneidau, Herbert. *Sacred Discontent: The Bible in Western Tradition*. Berkeley: University of California Press, 1976.

Searle, John R. "The Mission of the University." *Academic Questions* 7 (Winter 1993-94): 80-85.

Shah, Idries, ed. and trans. *The Way of the Sufi*. London: Arkana, 1968.

Shapira, Kalonymus Kalman. *A Student's Obligation*. Translated by Micha Odenheimer. Northvale, N.J.: Aronson, 1991.

Shestov, Lev. *Afiny i Ierusalim*. Paris: YMCA Press, 1951.

Sophocles. *Oedipus Rex*. Translated by Dudley Fitts and Robert Fitzgerald. In *The Oedipus Cycle*. New York: Harcourt Brace Jovanovitch, 1939.

Steinsaltz, Adin. *The Essential Talmud*. Translated by Chaya Galai. New York: Basic Books, 1976.

Steinsaltz, Adin. *Teshuvah: A Guide for the Newly Observant Jew*. New York: Free Press, 1987.

Steinsaltz, Adin. *The Long Shorter Way: Discourses on Chasidic Thought*. Translated by Yehuda Hanegbi. Northvale, N.J.: Aronson, 1988. a

Steinsaltz, Adin. *The Strife of the Spirit*. Northvale, N.J.: Aronson, 1988. b

Steinsaltz, Adin. *The Sustaining Utterance: Discourses on Chasidic Thought*. Edited and translated by Yehuda Hanegbi. Northvale, N.J.: Aronson, 1989.

Tolstoy, Leo. *The Death of Ivan Ilych and Other Stories*. Translated by Aylmer Maude and J.D. Duff. New York: Penguin, 1960.

Tolstoy, Leo. *Resurrection*. Translated by Rosemary Edmonds. New York: Penguin, 1981.

Tolstoy, Leo. *Confession.* Translated by David Patterson. New York: W.W. Norton, 1983.

Weinreich, Max. *Hitler's Professors: The Part of Scholarship in Germany's Crimes Against the Jewish People.* New York: Yiddish Scientific Institute, 1946.

Wiesel, Elic. *The Gates of the Forest.* Translated by Frances Frenaye. New York: Holt, Rinehart and Winston, 1966.

Wiesel, Elie. *A Beggar in Jerusalem.* Translated by Lily Edelman and Elie Wiesel. New York: Random House, 1970. a

Wiesel, Elie. *One Generation After.* New York: Pocket Books, 1970. b

Wiesel, Elie. *Ani Maamin: A Song Lost and Found Again.* Translated by Marion Wiesel. New York: Random House, 1973. a

Wiesel, Elie. *The Oath.* Translated by Marion Wiesel. New York: Avon, 1973. b

Wiesel, Elie. *Messengers of God: Biblical Portraits and Legends.* Translated by Marion Wiesel. New York: Random House, 1976.

Wiesel, Elie. *A Jew Today.* Translated by Marion Wiesel. New York: Random House, 1978.

Wiesel, Elie. *Night.* Translated by Stella Rodway. New York: Bantam, 1982. a

Wiesel, Elie. *Paroles d'etranger.* Paris: Editions du Seuil, 1982. b

Wiesel, Elie. *Against Silence: The Voice and Vision of Elie Wiesel.* Edited by Irving Abrahamson. 3 Vols. New York: Holocaust Library, 1985.

Wiesel, Elie. *From the Kingdom of Memory: Reminiscences.* New York: Summit, 1990.

Wiesel, Elie. *Sages and Dreamers.* Translated by Marion Wiesel. New York: Summit, 1991.

Wiesel, Elie, and de Saint-Cheron, Philippe. *Evil and Exile.* Translated by Jon Rothschild. Notre Dame, Ind.: University of Notre Dame Press, 1990.

Wiesel, Elie, and Cardinal O'Connor, John. *A Journey of Faith.* New York: Donald I. Fine, 1990.

Wiesenthal, Simon. *The Sunflower.* Translated by H.A. Piehler. New York: Schocken, 1976.

Wildavsky, Aaron. "Politically Correct Hiring." *Academic Questions* 7 (Winter 1993-94): 77-79.

Zalman, Schneur. *Likutei Amarim Tanya.* Translated by Nissan Mindel et al. Brooklyn: Kehot, 1981.

The Zohar. Translated by Harry Sperling and Maurice Simon. 5 Vols. London: Soncino, 1984.

ABOUT THE AUTHOR

David Patterson was born in 1948 in Bartlesville, Oklahoma. He attended Oklahoma State University, the University of Oklahoma, and the University of Oregon. He received a B.A. in philosophy (1972), and an M.A. (1976) and a Ph.D. (1978) in comparative literature.

Having taught in the public schools of the U.S. Virgin Islands, Patterson was appointed to his first university teaching position at the University of Oregon in 1978. In 1982 he accepted a position at Oklahoma State University, where he has taught in the departments of English, philosophy, and foreign languages and has served as director of the University Honors Program. In 1992 Patterson was the Visiting Sutton Chair in the Humanities at the University of Oklahoma, after which he returned to Oklahoma State University, where he currently is a professor of Russian and European literatures.

Patterson is the author of more than 70 articles and seven previous books, including *Faith and Philosophy* (1982), *The Affirming Flame: Religion, Language, Literature* (1988), *Literature and Spirit: Essays on Bakhtin* (1988), *In Dialogue and Dilemma with Elie Wiesel* (1991), *The Shriek of Silence: A Phenomenology of the Holocaust Novel* (1992), *Pilgrimage of a Proselyte: From Auschwitz to Jerusalem* (1993), and *Exile: The Sense of Alienation in Modern Russian Letters* (1995).

David Patterson and his wife, Geraldine, are the parents of two daughters, Miriam and Rachel.